IN THE BYWAYS OF LIFE

IN THE BYWAYS
OF LIFE

By

Stephen J. Brown, S.J.

The Reading Room.

THE TALBOT PRESS LIMITED

EIGHTY-NINE TALBOT STREET, DUBLIN

FIRST PUBLISHED 1952

De Facultate Superiorum Ordinis

Dublini, die 25 Julii 1952

THOMAS BYRNE, S.J.

Praep. Prov. Hiberniae Soc. Jesu

Nihil Obstat:

MICHAEL CLARKE,

Censor Theol. Deput.

Imprimi Potest:

✠ IOANNES CAROLUS,

Archiep. Dublinen.,

Hiberniae Primas.

DUBLINI, die 25° Octobris, 1952

Printed in the Republic of Ireland at the Talbot Press, Dublin

DEDICATION

To Fellow-Wayfarers in the Byways

wishing them

Godspeed on Their Way

ACKNOWLEDGMENTS

MY thanks are due to the Editors of *The Catholic World*, *The Review for Religious*, and the *Irish Rosary* for permission to reproduce articles which appeared in their respective periodicals, viz., " Contentment ", and " The Cynic " in the first-named, " Patience " in the second, and " The Sere and Yellow Leaf " ? in the third. All the other contents of the book now appear for the first time.

BY WAY OF INTRODUCTION

POLITICS, Economics, Sociology, Finance, Philosophy, Theology, all the sciences from Paleontology and Archæology to the latest discoveries in radio-activity and the much-talked-of atomic and hydrogen bombs. All these things are important—unquestionably, portentously important. One can imagine them as lofty, impressive-looking, if somewhat forbidding, buildings ranged along the highways of life. Important people, select and expert men and women, go in and out. But many an ordinary passer-by gazes up at them with a certain awe, and never ventures to enter. And many others wend their way through such hidden and lowly byways that they barely glimpse these towering structures. They go by the little roads and the country lanes, passing by a cottage here and there or a rural village, through green hedgerows with gates that open up vistas of field and valley and woodland. Some, even, there are who dwell in great cities but who live as strangers and sojourners there, not concerning themselves with the activities for which the mighty buildings have been reared and knowing naught of them.

What I am putting into this book will bear much the same relation to those subjects of portentous and indubitable importance which I have set down above as do the sights and incidents, the cottages and villages of byways and country lanes to the great buildings of the city. But the things to be spoken of in these pages are not therefore wholly without importance. For the days and hours not only of unimportant but of quite important people are filled with little things, unconsidered trifles that go to make our lives and that may make or mar our happiness. The politician, the financier, the company director, the philosopher, the scientist, not to say the ' eminent physician ' and the ' learned judge ' are also *men*, and so sons and brothers, husbands and fathers, and much else besides. In these latter capacities they may possibly find something to interest them in the somewhat unlearned and unscientific considerations that shall be put forward in this book.

In a former book named *Studies in Life By and Large* I set down some thoughts about matters that might interest people just as men and women, matters such as the art of making allowances, the crowd-mind, the spirit of little children, the search for happiness, the meaning of life, and so forth. Well, here are further thoughts set down in a similar vein, but less elaborately. They are, I hope, unpretentious. Yet I would not have it thought that they are " written-down " to the level of " the meanest intelligence ". That would be the merest affectation. People of " meanest intelligence ", whoever they be, do not read such books, and would profit but little if they did. On the other hand, these chapters have no claim to be either deep or exhaustive. All the writer aims at is to set going in the reader's mind trains of thought which may possibly prove to be of some help or comfort to him as he goes on his way through the byways of life.

CONTENTS

CHAPTER		PAGE
	By Way of Introduction	IX
I	Minor Joys by the Wayside	1
II	On the Tragi-Comedy of being One's Self ..	17
III	On Making the most of One's Self	26
IV	On the Defects of One's Qualities	39
V	Two Virtues of the Byways	
	Patience	53
	Contentment	58
VI	Fellow-Wayfarers	
	The Cynic	69
	The Pessimist	76
	The Conversationalist	82
	Companions and Comrades	88
VII	Ruts in the Byways	93
VIII	Of Musts and the Second Mile	107
IX	Lonely Spots in the Byways	113
X	Hardship in the Byways: Some Thoughts on Crosses	121
XI	Homely Wisdom from the Byways	128
XII	"The Sere and Yellow Leaf"?	139
	Epilogue	148
	Appendix A. Books on Self-Development ..	150
	Appendix B. Some Further Notes	158

IN THE BYWAYS OF LIFE

◆

CHAPTER I

MINOR JOYS BY THE WAYSIDE

*" Always to be happy is an art, and not a very difficult
one. It consists merely of training oneself to perceive,
appreciate, and thankfully utilize little joys."*
PAUL WILHELM VON KEPPLER, Bishop of Rothenburg.

I SHOULD like to be able to endorse without reserve this
interesting saying. Undoubtedly there is much truth in
it, but I wonder if the attainment and maintenance of
happiness here below is quite such a simple thing as
the good Bishop seems to say. Anyhow the perception,
appreciation, and utilization of little joys (in accordance
with his adage) is my theme at the moment. I should
be glad if I could help you to see that they can be
enjoyed as easily in the byways as on the great highways
of life.

I

The early years of the children of the very poor,
though full of hardship and privations, rendered endu-
rable only by use and wont and because they have known
nothing better, are brightened by very simple things—
a rag doll, a tin can, a chariot of old boxes, a cast-off
rubber wheel, above all a ball of any sort whatever.
These are their joys and give more pure delight than the
most expensive toys of wealthy children. Indeed, so far
as the ball and the wheel are concerned, these are joys
to rich and poor alike—from the old rubber ball of the

1

poor child through football, cricket ball, tennis ball,
hand ball, hurling ball, to the golf ball of the professional
classes; and again from the child's hoop to the boy's—
and girl's—bicycle, and on to the motor-car, the grown
man's plaything. Who will ever calculate the sum of
undiluted pleasure that these simple things have given
to young and old?

I wonder whether in later life there are any joys to
equal certain joys of our youth, the joy of scoring a
brilliant goal or a brilliant try, of making top score for
one's side and " carrying one's bat ", of carrying off the
winning set after a hotly contested match against an
almost equal opponent. If there be, the writer for one
has not known them.

Games are but one example of what is, perhaps, the
greatest source of pleasure we mortals possess—the
congenial exercise of our powers and faculties, or of our
skill, be it congenital or acquired. As the game goes
on there is every scope for suppleness and strength
of limb, quickness of eye, speed, cleverness of many
kinds, skill acquired by training and practice. Given
abounding health, the exhilaration of vigorous exercise,
and the fresh open air, what better joy could youth
demand?

But all this applies to *playing* games. Looking on at
them is another matter. This within my own lifetime
has grown from trifling, to enormous, proportions. Vast
crowds now gather from far and near to look on at an
important match. Yet it is safe to say that of the multitude of onlookers very few indeed play the game they
look at or indeed any games at all. Games tend more
and more to be played only by the highly skilled, the
exceptional experts, though the final stage may be still
pretty far off. One is reminded of an amusing illustration that appeared in a humorous journal. It depicts
two tiny boys playing marbles in the centre of an arena,

surrounded by hundreds of spectators, all registering intense interest and excitement. And no wonder, for it was the final of the National Marbles Union! As Chesterton wrote, speaking of games in general: " As long as the game was a game, everybody wanted to join in it. When it becomes an art, everybody wants to look at it." (¹) And now it has become a business. Seeing the multitudes on their way to a football match, one is tempted to think that the young people among them would be better off playing any sort of outdoor game, however badly, and their elders the better for almost any other form of relaxation. But, no doubt, the question is not so simple as that, and yelling on the touchline for an hour or two is at all events a harmless occupation, and the working classes have few alternatives.

It is remarkable how many forms of recreation nowadays are *passive*—looking on at games or races, listening-in to the radio, watching films in the cinemas, even being carried about in motor cars. All these are good in their way, at least as occasional relaxations. In addition, they may be useful and instructive. I am not forgetting Wordsworth's " wise passiveness " and " the harvest of a quiet eye ". Nor do I wish to take back anything that I wrote in a previous book about what it means to look at life through poet's eyes.(²) But I think that in respect of our present theme, these amusements fall short. They do not give the same unfailing joy as *active*

(¹) " The wholly disproportionate attention given to games in our talk and in our country's Press shows that they have largely lost their right place in the art of living; they have ceased to be games." J. W. Coutts: *The Art of Living* (London, 1929).

The great national games are a dispiriting study. . . . They are now mostly composed of a few skilled players who are paid to play, and tens of thousands of onlookers who pay to be amused. Yet to be amused is passive; not active nor creative in form and function. But to " play " bears an active meaning or reminiscence.

Father Vincent McNabb, O.P., in *The Wayside* (1915).

(²) *Studies in Life By and Large.* Chapter VI.

recreations. Nor do they to the same extent provide the congenial exercise of our powers and faculties, abilities and skill.

I should very much like to quote here in full an excellent chapter, "Games" (xv) in A. C. Benson's *From a College Window*, as admirably setting forth views that I believe to be sound. Instead I shall quote this vigorous passage from a distinguished writer, Ross J. S. Hoffman, author of *The Will to Freedom*, *Tradition and Progress*, etc., etc.: "It is my belief that sport, not religion, has been the 'opiate of the people', in the last twenty years. Abroad and at home sport has virtually ceased to be sporting; it has been commercialized, politicized, totalitarianized, and even raised to the level of a religion: the cult of physical culture, an abominable and soul killing heresy. In my opinion carousing in a tavern is far less bad for young men than this sober new puritanism of keeping fit." Perhaps Mr. Hoffman overstates his case a little. But G. K. Chesterton, in *All Things Considered* ("Patriotism and Sport") says much the same in his genial way.

To a far less degree I think than open air games is what is collectively known as 'sport' an exercise of one's powers and faculties. 'Sports', no doubt, are exercises of speed, strength, and agility, as in the 'games' of ancient Greece. But 'sport' more often means looking on at horses or dogs racing, of which the gain to the onlooker is more than dubious, or else hunting and shooting. To multitudes of people sport means two men pummelling and battering one another, often in an orgy of blood, with ever-present danger of life-long injury, and even of death. It would, however, be absurd for the present writer to pass judgment on any of these things, from one at least of which he derived long ago the keenest enjoyment. But anyhow they hardly come within what he means by minor joys.

Neither do what we may roughly describe as *amusements*—cinema, theatres,[1] parties, shows of all kinds, receptions, entertainments, dances, house parties. None of these things are evil in themselves; to say the contrary would be puritanical. But surely they ought to be exceptions, occasional relaxations, not the warp and woof of life. And that, of course, is supposing that they are not of the wholly frivolous, boisterous, or sensuous kind, mere excitement of the nerves. But at best they leave us where they found us, not fitter for the work of life, not more robust in health, nor braced in spirit. Their sole aftermath, too often, is headache, frayed nerves, a sense of discontent with drab surroundings and monotonous labour, and it may be a troubled conscience.

It may be worth while to pause here for a moment and ask ourselves what we mean by joy and what we mean by pleasure. Though often either word is used for the other, they do not really mean the same thing. We speak of the pleasures of the table but hardly of its joys. We speak of the joy of a good conscience but hardly of its pleasure. Pleasure, even when quite lawful, is on a lower plane than joy. It is a condition of the senses and appetites, while joy affects the heart and mind. Animals no doubt feel pleasure, but it would be queer to talk of them as full of joy, unless we are using a figure of speech. In the midst of bodily pain and suffering, joy may still abide with us, as when the Apostles after their scourging " went forth rejoicing that they had been accounted worthy to suffer dishonour for the Name "[2]. Pleasures may give joy, but not all pleasures do: a round of pleasures and amusements may leave the heart and the mind empty and joyless. They can do little to comfort sorrow or to banish loneliness.

---

[1] I am thinking of the common run of films, the plays in second-rate theatres, " variety ", and music halls.

[2] Acts V. 40-42.

> Though pleasure fire the maddened brain,
> The heart, the heart is lonely still [1]

Pleasures satiate and pall, but we can never have enough of joy. It is surely of pleasures rather than of joys that Milton was thinking in the opening of *Il Penseroso:*

> Hence vain deluding Joys,
> The brood of folly without father bred,
> How little you bestead
> Or fill the fixéd mind with all your toys!

It is of course true that pleasures are often ' deluding '. But there are pleasures and pleasures—pleasures that give real joy, however transient, and pleasures that are merely frivolous and profitless when they are not dangerous and even evil. Joy, on the other hand, is the very spirit of Christianity. The contrast, even from a purely natural point of view, between joy and pleasure, is set forth in this little poem by a modern poet:

JOY AND PLEASURE

By WILLIAM H. DAVIES

> Now Joy is born of parents poor,
>   And Pleasure of our richer kind:
> Though Pleasure's free she cannot sing
>   As sweet a song as Joy confined.
>
> Pleasure's a Moth, that sleeps by day
>   And dances by false glare at night:
> But Joy's a butterfly, that loves
>   To spread its wings in Nature's light.
>
> Joy's like a Bee that gently sucks
>   Away on blossoms its sweet hour:
> But Pleasure's like a greedy Wasp,
>   That plums and cherries would devour.

---

[1] I quote from memory and do not even remember who was the author of the lines.

A

Joy's like a Lark that lives alone,
    Whose ties are very strong, though few:
But Pleasure like a cuckoo roams,
    Makes much acquaintance, no friends true.

Joy from her heart doth sing at home,
    With little care if others hear;
But Pleasure then is cold and dumb,
    And sings and laughs with strangers near.

Having in mind the *British* working classes, a recent writer speaks thus of the amusements of the people:

" Starved of life the worker takes make-believe from the cinema, stimulation over the bar, petty excitement at greyhound races, a gamble from the street bookmaker and the football pool, a relief in boisterous laughter or too-sweet sentiment at the music-hall. He squanders loose change in amusement parks. A penny in the slot and Old Mother Shipton will tell a young fellow his fortune. Another penny will give him six metal balls with which he is invited to try for fantastic scores on the gaudily illuminated pin-tables. For 20,000 he may win the prize of two cigarettes. Or he may just use up precious time. At home you have to puzzle over crossword puzzles just to fill up empty time. Or, a little bit better employed, you may listen to the wireless pouring in your ears sequences of jazz and comedy, or answering questions to which it does not know the answers. Then there is the fascinating game of bridge and the no less fascinating game of poker . . . avid devourers of time and energy. . . ."[1]

Yes, does it not all seem a waste of this little life given us here below for greater ends? And how little real joy is the outcome of it all?

---

[1] Stephen Graham : *Thinking of Living* (London : Benn, 1949), p. 13.

B

Considering in a general way the pleasures and amusements of to-day—such of them as are in themselves harmless, I think we shall not be far wrong in saying that they are good unless and until they become a mania or a craze—a craze for motoring, for card-playing, for looking on at games and sports, for detective fiction, for dancing, smoking, drinking, for the " pictures ". It is when these things become a craze that they become harmful. And when may they be said to have become a craze? Obviously when they interfere with duty or with one's life work. But also, I submit, when they squeeze out, so to speak, and substitute themselves for, better things, things better intellectually, socially, morally, religiously. For the things I have mentioned have commonly no value whatever except as an occasional distraction or relaxation. Moreover, they may easily cause worse damage to a man or woman than merely the wasting of time given them for better things.

One partial exception must, I think, be made, and it is in favour of the films. One may agree with Father Lord when he says that he regards a good motion picture not only as one of the most satisfying forms of entertainment but as a high dramatic experience. It can, he says, be a lesson in history, national characteristics, character, the classics in literature and drama. And that is certainly true. But only of the relatively rare good pictures. Indiscriminate and frequent picture-going is a very different matter. To quote a thoughtful writer in a recent book ([1]): " If the young went to films rarely and selectively there would be little harm, but there is bitter and destructive harm in their going—and, indeed, in anyone's going—twice or three times a week to a programme selected for them ", even if that programme contains neither gangsterism nor a profanation of sex.

([1]) Charles Morgan : *Liberties of the Mind*, p. 50.

For gradually they come to live imaginatively in an unreal world and to lose their independent thinking powers. The films become for them a form of dope. All this and more, Father Lord, whom I have quoted in favour of good films, goes on to say in similar terms.

It will seem very old-fashioned, no doubt, to quote Goldsmith in praise of the simpler joys. Yet I venture to set down the following short passage as expressing better what I feel myself than I can express it:

> Yes, let the rich deride, the proud disdain
> These simple pleasures of the lowly train,
> To me more dear, congenial to my heart
> One native charm than all the gloss of art;
> Spontaneous joys where Nature has its play
> The soul adopts and owns their first-born sway;
> Lightly they frolic o'er the vacant (¹) mind,
> Unenvy'd, unmolested, unconfined.

II

And now that we have somewhat cleared the ground, we may go on to consider a few of those minor joys which I had in mind when thinking over this chapter. There is, of course, nothing new about any of them. But precisely for that very reason we are apt to pass them by or leave them in the shadow. And to save repetition of *experto crede*, let me say at the outset that nearly every one of these sources of joy have been at one time or another a joy to the writer.

It is good to go to exhibitions and galleries and look at pictures, to go to concerts and recitals and listen to good music. It is, however, not too much to say that these things are for the privileged few. But what of *practising* these arts? Most children scrawl crude designs on paper and daub them with paint: nearly all of them

---

(¹) By " vacant " Goldsmith meant unoccupied, viz., by anxious and importunate thought, or, as we might express it to-day, thoroughly relaxed.

progress no further. A little teaching would make their sketching and painting a joy for life, as it was for a certain period of my own. Again there is the *practice* of music. My own tuition ended at the age of twelve, but the exercise of the very imperfect skill thus acquired was an unfailing joy for fifty years thereafter. I see you formulate in your mind the unspoken question, 'But was it a joy for the hearers?' Well, I fear it would hardly have been a joy had there been any hearers! But whereas elements of drawing can be taught to anybody, it is not so, I think, with music. Many have not the requisite 'ear', and many would have in after life no opportunity of practising the art. If you cannot learn to play some instrument, follow the advice of a wise counsellor and " try at all costs to cultivate, for joy's sake, an appreciation of good music ".[1]

Then there is the simple joy, despised by most in these days of hurry, of walking, in company or alone, in the countryside. If alone, one can take for companion-ship a favourite book, reading as the fancy takes one, or stopping to observe some aspect of nature, wandering now on roads, now across the fields or in country lanes, now by dawn-light

> To hear the lark begin his flight
> And singing startle the dull night
> From his watch-tower in the skies
> Till the dappled dawn doth rise. . . .
> Sometimes walking not unseen
> By hedge-row elms, on hillocks green
> Right against the eastern gate
> Where the great sun begins his state
> Robed in flames and amber light. . . .

A spectacle, I fear, witnessed by few but the early milkers. Or again, in the quiet of the evening, seeing

> Such sights as youthful poets dream
> On summer eves by haunted stream. . . .

[1] Father J. G. Vance in *Sources of Enjoyment* (The Grail).

It may seem prosaic to pass from such romantic rambles to the humble bicycle. Yet I wonder if there may be found on earth a happier being than a boy on his first bicycle. And though in after years it chiefly fulfils a modest role as a means of transport, it can be, as for the present writer during more than fifty years, the instrument of many a happy day and hour.

Then there is boating. To me it has always been a delight in all its forms. Rowing on the Suir or the Corrib, the Barrow, or the Brosna, on the sea, and once alone on Derwentwater: sailing in Bantry Bay or Lough Corrib or, again, on the sea or even on the Grand Canal: in motor boats to the Saltees or the Skelligs or Inismurray or the islands in Lough Corrib. Opportunities have been few and far between, but delightful when they came. And the possibilities are endless.

And then there is swimming, still a pleasure at three score years and ten.

Among the instincts that are proper to human nature is one that for want of a better name we may call the ' creative ' instinct, the urge to make things. The activity of this instinct, like the exercise of all our powers, is a source of joy. The child delights in its crude efforts at drawing and painting as, later, the artist will rejoice in his ' creations '. It is, I venture to think, a real asset in life to be taught a handicraft. That has not been the writer's fortune,(1) for his has been in the main a life of study and of teaching, his only ' creations ' being articles and books. There are scores of simple handicrafts and scores of books to teach the amateur how to practise them. Needlework, embroidery, knitting, and the like can play in woman's life the role of such handicrafts for boys. There is another form of creation which

---

(1) An exception being the practice, during a brief period, of fretwork. One might try other woodwork, poker work, modelling, handweaving, bookbinding, or just plain carpentry.

the writer, likewise, has had no opportunity of practising
—gardening, not hiring a number of men to do the work
it involves, but taking spade and trowel and barrow and
doing it, or much of it, oneself. Only thus will you
create a ' thing of beauty ', all your own, and feel that
it is 'a joy for ever'. A writer([1]) already quoted calls
gardening " one of the serenest joys on earth ".

Almost equally ' serene ' and a joy for thousands
everywhere, is angling, not deep-sea fishing, nor trawling,
nor netting, but just casting a fly to lure a foolish fish,
as practised by the writer long ago in Wicklow mountain
streams and Connemara lakes. As somebody has said:
" It does not seem to make sense, but a man who is
worrying himself to death can go fishing along a mountain stream and suddenly realize that he has not a care
in the world ".

I think it sound advice that early in life one ought
to open as many doors as possible, doors opening upon
sources of interest and perhaps of joy. In other words,
it is a good thing to cultivate a variety of interests. They
will help to fill pleasantly one's hours of leisure and they
will be an asset after retirement from one's life-work and
for the years of old age. Some of these interests will be,
it is to be hoped, definitely serious—some work of zeal
or charity. At the moment, however, my theme is *minor*
joys, and it is because these interests may yet be sources
of joy that I am suggesting their cultivation. One who
took this piece of advice was able to write a few years
later:

> " I believe that doing things for yourself is the
> vital component for a sound personality and an
> exciting life. In the past two years I have done
> fifty or more oil paintings, most of them bad. I
> have written a little poetry and read a great deal
> more. I have baked everything from a loaf of bread

([1]) Father John G. Vance.

to a meat pie. I have studied Spanish and geology.
And, because I have four children, I have also fished,
skated, played football, made snowmen, played
badminton. Meanwhile I have held down a full-
time newspaper job ".(¹)

On the other hand, in the course of conversation a
short time ago, one who for many years had held an
important position told me that he was about to retire,
that he had no other interest in the world than the work
from which he was retiring, and that now he was utterly
at a loss as to what to do with his life.

I have not yet mentioned another source of minor
joys, of joys which make up for their minuteness by
their multiplicity—hobbies, from the boy's stamp album
or autograph book to the collector's antique porcelain
or Aldine editions. To those who engage in them they
give, if nothing else, a spice of interest in life. And they
are so various as to provide something for every taste—
photography, botanising, birds, bibliomania, coins, bees,
languages, etc., etc.: and then collecting, it matters little
what. The writer's hobby has been bibliography, the
collection of titles of books, which, to collectors of other
things, will seem as dull an occupation as to him the
collecting of—those other things. What matters it, so
only the object be pursued with zest and captured with
excitement and joy, like that of the woman in the parable
who found her lost groat and called in the neighbours
to celebrate. And then, if we may venture to include
them among hobbies, multifarious are the objects of
study that may occupy our hours of leisure, from any
of the physical sciences, through various types and phases
of literature, to philosophy and theology. Why not make
yourself an authority on some favourite author or some
period of history? Anyhow, if you would banish bore-
dom once for all, cultivate an absorbing hobby.

(¹) T. E. Murphy in *The Reader's Digest*.

All that has been said may go a little way at least towards solving what has come to be known as the Problem of the Use of Leisure. This is to a great extent a modern problem simply because in our days a vastly greater number of people have leisure than ever before, or rather than since the beginning of the nineteenth century and its industrial revolution. And periods of leisure are still growing in duration. As Viscount Samuel expressed it in a recent address (¹): " Wisely the community decides to devote a larger share of the growing usufruct of productive power to lessening the proportion of men's lives that is devoted to earning the means of living, and in increasing the proportion given to the enjoyment of life itself. And the life is more than the livelihood and the workman more than the work ".

It is, above all, the working classes that have benefited by this movement through shorter daily working hours, a shorter week, and paid holidays. Retirement is earlier and longevity increasing. Taking the pensionable age as 65 for men and 60 for women, there were in England, in 1901, two-and-a-quarter millions of such people. By 1941 this number had risen to five-and-a-half millions. As to paid holidays, the number of people for whom provision had to be made in the holiday season of 1947 was thirty millions.

Naturally, the solution of so vast a problem has called forth great efforts on the part not only of individuals but of local authorities and of the State itself. Typical of the literature it has given rise to is such a book as *The Problem of Leisure*, by H. W. Durant (London: Routledge, 1938), treating the subject as a problem of the machine age. But we of the byways may well leave this problem, like so many others, to be solved by the sociologists and the planners, by local and central govern-

---

(¹) *Leisure in a Democracy*, a speech delivered before, and subsequently published by, the National Book League, 1949.

ment, in short, by the great ones who dwell on the highways. We of the byways would do well to make use,
according to our individual tastes, of the institutions those
others may be good enough to create for us—their play-
grounds and rest-gardens, playing fields, parks, green
belts, clubs and associations—athletic, social, musical,
dramatic, their camps and recreation centres, hostels and
swimming pools, and all the rest. We in Ireland might
well ask ourselves what, in these respects, we have created
for the people. What we *might* create is set forth in a
pamphlet published in 1944, *Planning for Leisure*, by
Noel Moffet.[1]

But minor joys, whatever they be, are merely the spice
of life, not life itself any more than salt and pepper are
a meal. As the poet said, and, however hackneyed the
quotation, it is worth repeating:

> Not enjoyment and not sorrow
> Is our destined end or way.

Neither of these things is the business of life. Minor
joys are helps along the byways, and sorrow part of the
way of the cross which every Christian must tread. Men
and women must earn their living here below by honest
toil, and life eternal by carrying out their allotted tasks.
This is the substance of life.

*   *   *   *

If you would care to read more about the element of
joy in our Christian lives, I can recommend to you
More Joy, by Bishop Keppler (St. Louis: Herder). It
is old-fashioned, if you like, it is solid, but nearly everything worth saying on the subject is to be found in it.
And as regards leisure, you may acquire for a few pence
a pamphlet published in St. Louis (The Queen's Work)
and in Ireland by the Catholic Truth Society—*Your*

---

[1] Dublin : Duffy.

New Leisure and How to Use It, by Daniel A. Lord, S.J. This is an excellent piece of writing, full of practical suggestions.

A Note about Other Joys

The reader of the preceding chapter might not unreasonably wonder why the writer of it has not spoken of certain other joys. The answer is twofold—first, he had no notion of being exhaustive in his mention of joys : he has even omitted something which to him has been an unfailing joy—poetry.   Secondly, he set out to speak only of *minor* joys.   And so he did not mention, for instance, the joy of a good conscience to which the *Imitation of Christ* devotes a chapter,([1]) nor the joy of being kind to others and especially of giving gifts.   Still less could he mention among minor joys the deep perennial wellsprings of Christian joy—the Fatherhood of God, the Brotherhood of Christ, the indwelling of the Holy Spirit, and Our Lady, ' Cause of Our Joy '.

([1]) Book II. Ch. 6.

CHAPTER II

ON THE TRAGI-COMEDY OF BEING ONESELF

In all your wanderings round this world of care, whether in byways or on highways, have you ever met a person who was exactly and in every respect like yourself? Whoever you may happen to be, I think you will have to answer, No! Put the same question to as many persons as you may care to interrogate, and the answer is sure to be the same. The fact is, though so much is said, written, and done as though human beings were as like as ninepins, we are all different from one another: each one of us is peculiar, nay, in a sense, unique.

It is worth while dwelling a little on these manifold differences between one human being and another, for, though they may be vaguely admitted in principle, they are often ignored in practice. First there are the physical differences—eyes of varying power from keenest eyesight to blindness, an acutely differential sense of smell or practically none at all, endless varieties in tone and timbre of voice, so that one can very often know people from scores of others by their voices alone; facial features, from the subtle differences between 'identical' twins, to the difference between faces that are almost animal and faces that are almost angelic. How easily conflicts may arise from these mere physical differences, what tragedies a fair face has caused throughout human history from the face of Helen of Troy—or the beauty of Deirdre of the Sorrows, or of Queen Cleopatra, even to *crimes passionels* in our own days.

> I had great beauty: ask thou not my name:
> No one can be more wise than destiny.
> Many drew swords and died.   Where'er I came
> I brought calamity.

So Tennyson wrote in his *Dream of Fair Women*.
Yet such obvious physical features are not the principal
sources of difference. All doctors know in what endless
ways the constitution of one patient differs from another's.
There are differences in needs—of sleep, or food, or
recreation, differences in reaction to noise, or monotony,
or fatigue, to heat and cold. One person is, as we say,
' a bundle of nerves ', another frankly unable to understand what nerves really mean. One man is allergic to
this or that, the next not in the least. What's one man's
meat is another man's poison.

How endlessly people differ in their tastes! To one,
music may be ecstasy, to another it means nothing: as
we say, he has not a note in his head. And so it is with
the visual arts, with natural scenery, with poetry. For
these things many a man and woman has no use. Their
tastes and likings tend to quite different objects. Tastes
in food are equally various. The tastes of some people
make others foolishly angry. It is wiser to shrug one's
shoulders and turn for comfort to the time-honoured
adage—"There's no accounting for tastes", *de gustibus
non est disputandum*.

Mental faculties, gifts, and aptitudes show endless
variety. Take only the memory. There is on the one
hand the memory of a Macaulay who remembered whatever caught his fancy without going through the process
of consciously getting it by heart,(¹) or the amazing memory
of an expert pianist playing a sonata or a concerto without

(¹) Once while waiting for his father during an afternoon call he read
through Scott's *Lay of the Last Minstrel*.   On his return home he recited for
his mother as many of the cantos as she cared to listen to.   He once said
that if by some miracle all copies of *Paradise Lost* and the *Pilgrim's Progress*
were destroyed he could undertake to reproduce them from memory.   Some

the Score, and on the other the memories of so many of us, lamenting that ours is like a sieve, unable to retain anything we put into it; names and dates and quotations will not come to mind when we want them. Some people have notably feeble intelligence and prodigious memories. One feeble-minded youth memorized the telephone directory of his town and many car numbers of its citizens, and could quote them on request. People in certain avocations develop astonishing memories for their particular businesses. Some people seem to be born mathematicians while others can hardly add up a column of figures without a blunder. Some people are brilliant, or at all events exuberant, conversationalists, while we are tongue-tied. Some who are dunces in book-learning have remarkable aptitudes in other directions: their abilities may seem to be rather in their hands than in their heads, and yet what can the hands do without the directing brain?

When men and women are thrown together in business, in sports, in the home, differences show themselves. One likes fresh air and another hates draughts; one likes to listen to the radio and another wants it turned off, or if they must listen, one wants music, another politics, and a third the sporting news. And so with all the other details of daily life.

The existence of all these manifold differences between one person and another surely goes to show for one thing the absurdity of education carried out on a mass-production basis, with little or no attempt to help the pupils to find out their individual aptitudes. But that is only said in passing.

What is more to our present point is this: Each human being is a mixture of many (some psychologists say as

---

things that he read he could repeat verbatim forty years later. These and many other examples of his memory are related in Trevelyan's biography, Chapter I.

many as three hundred) distinct abilities, tendencies, and traits, any of which may be possessed in a vast variety of degrees. To each one of us God has given a self endowed with a certain combination of these qualities, aptitudes, abilities—call them what we will, and it is this combination, this bunch or bouquet of gifts, qualities, etc., that constitutes what nowadays we call our personality. One may not have what is called a striking personality, a remarkable personality, or a very original personality, but personality of some sort every one must have, because personality is simply *one's spiritual nature considered as individualized in oneself*, in this particular self which is our own.

Now, there are people who look about them and observe on all sides other people with gifts that they themselves do not possess, cleverer people, more brilliant people, people gifted with wonderful imagination, with most retentive memories, with skills of various kinds. And they are filled with a sense of tragedy when they contemplate their own lack of so many powers and gifts, their poor memory, their want of imagination, their utter inability to follow certain lines of activity and accomplish what others have accomplished. They forget that all those whose accomplishments they look upon with envy have their own limitations, their own lack of aptitude for many things. History has no record of any man who had a genius for everything or was an expert in everything. Such people are nowhere to be found, for every man is finite and has his limitations. Nay, the greatest geniuses have often the most astonishing limitations. They often have, as we shall presently see, the defects of their very qualities. And here by the way comes in an element of the comic. A classic example was Samuel Johnson, a really great and also a very good man after his own fashion. He was almost unbelievably eccentric. Macaulay it would seem, was hardly exaggerating when

he described the old Doctor's "scrofula, his St. Vitus's
dance, his rolling walk, his blinking eye, his insatiable
appetite for fish sauce and veal pie with plums, his
inextinguishable thirst for tea [twenty cups at a sitting],
his contortions, his mutterings, his gruntings, his
puffings" and so on. Great artists and composers,
great literary men, too, are often almost as remarkable
for their limitations as for their gifts. It is as if, to
counterbalance the greatness of one particular talent,
other if minor talents were denied them. Perhaps, even,
that line of Dryden is not a great exaggeration—

> Great wits are sure to madness near allied . . .

Is it really, then, all tragedy that your personality
should lack the great gifts of genius? Perhaps after all
your ' self ' has qualities of common sense, balance, and
practical ability in which people of genius may be
altogether lacking. So do not take your limitations *au
grand tragique*. Be sure that your Maker has given you
gifts at least sufficient for the *main* business of your lives,
which is concerned not with your brief span of life here
below but with the life that lies beyond.

We are, then, what we are: we are condemned to be
ourselves. That for the Godless existentialist, adherent of
the prevailing fashion in philosophy, is the central tragedy
of life. Yet one of their leaders in a far from humorous
book manages to see a comic side of it. His example is
a typical waiter whom he describes to the life.

"His whole manner is a performance. He is play-
acting: he is enjoying himself. What, then, is his role?
Whom is he impersonating? The answer is simple: he
is impersonating a waiter in a café. For many of us, no
doubt, all our life is play-acting."

So, when all is said, we must put up with the self we
have.([1]) One type of persons only can enjoy the (strictly

([1]) " There is a time ", writes Emerson, " in every man's education when
he arrives at the conviction that envy [of other men's gifts] is ignorance;

temporary) luxury of being somebody else—the actor.
And the actor, once he has ceased to "strut and fret his
hour upon the stage ", must go back to and put up with
his same old self. If, instead of bemoaning our tragic
fate because the self our Creator gave us is not to our
taste, or not equal to the measure of our ambitions, we
were to accept that self as a gift from His hands, how
much happier our lives could be. Self-pity is one of the
poorest forms of self-indulgence and an inferiority
complex is a serious handicap in life. St. Francis de Sales
has summed it all up in one perfect sentence: " Soyons
ce que nous sommes et soyons-le bien, pour faire honneur
au maître duquel nous sommes l'œuvre."(¹)

" A consulting psychologist ", writes Dr. H. Emerson
Fosdick, " told me recently that most cases of emotional
maladjustment are due to the fact that people will not
accept themselves. They resent their limitations. They
want to be someone else."

But it is by no means enough just to put up with our
self, our personality. We must actually defend it, and
that is not an easy task in these days of ours. Under
totalitarian régimes it must be very difficult indeed. For
there every citizen—I mean ' comrade '—is expected to
think exactly what the government wants him to think.
But even outside the iron curtains or barbed wire en-
tanglements of such régimes many influences combine to
suppress any individuality one may possess and reduce
everybody to a dead level of impersonality. Fashion,
convention, standardisation, propaganda, the party news-

that imitation is suicide; that he must take himself for better, for worse, as
his portion; that though the wide universe is full of good, no grain of
nourishing corn can come to him but through his toil bestowed on that plot
of ground which is given him to till." Not long ago there appeared a novel
by Julian Green in which the author contrives to show by tragedy that the
desire to be someone else is much better unfulfilled. The novel is entitled
If I Were You.

(¹) It is spoiled in translation, but here is the literal meaning: " Let us be
what we are and let us be that well, in order to be a credit to the Master
Craftsman whose handiwork we are."

paper, the best seller, the radio, the screen tell us what
we ought to think and what to feel about things. Many
people are frantically eager to think the standard
thoughts, accept the current opinions, and be in keeping
with the latest fashions: conformity is their ideal.
Anybody who does not conform is eccentric, an oddity,
or old-fashioned and out of date, which is even worse.

Now it is childish to seek to be different merely for the
sake of being different. Of people who do Pope writes—

> So much they scorn the crowd that if the throng
> By chance go right, they purposely go wrong.

A certain degree of conformity is incumbent on all of us.
But it is something worse than childish so to sink our
personality as to be ready to drift with every current of
opinion and veer like a weathercock with every breeze
of fashion, or, as St. Paul puts it, to allow ourselves to
be " tossed on the waves and carried around by every
wind of doctrine." Not for that did God give us an
intellect and judgment of our own.

Let me here transcribe for you a page from a thoughtful
German writer still living:(¹)

" Every one of us bears a primal image of his being
within himself—the Divine idea in which the Creator
thought that being. This embodies not only the universal
image of ' human-being ' but also all of what constitutes
a given individual personality. Each person exists only
once is in fact a ἅπαξ λεγόμενον (²) of God. The
being-human exists in this particular form only once ".
It follows, he goes on to say, that in order to be free a
man must emphasize this personal individuality in all
his being and acting—must live true to himself and
therefore to the Divine idea of that self. And here the
German writer meets the English poet speaking through
old Polonius—

(¹) Romano Guardini in Vom Sinn der Kirche.
(²) Said of a word or expression that occurs only once in an author's works.

c

> " To thine own self be true
> And it must follow as the night the day
> Thou canst not then be false to any man."

Nor yet to God, provided only that this self to which we are true is our *best* self, rising above our baser instincts and our trends towards evil. Let me adduce another and quite different witness to this truth. " If there be any meaning in human life at all ", writes Alfred Noyes, " and any foundation for religion, it is to be found in the value of the individual to himself, to the world, and to his Creator, as a ' single separate person ', possessing a unique quality, so that in the universal symphony, his own personal note is as necessary as any other, and, for its own particular purpose, is even a little better than any other."

But again, to defend and preserve our self, our personality, is still not enough. Our Maker did not give it to us to lock it up, like a museum piece, in a glass case and there admire it. He gave it to us that we might develop its abilities and powers, and, whether these amount to one talent or to ten, we must not act like the man in the parable who wrapped his single talent in a ' napkin ' and laid it aside till the coming of his lord. We know what was the Master's judgment on men of that type. Education is, or ought to be, the developing of personality. And education, far from ending with our last class in school or our last lecture in the university, ought to continue all our lives. True, whether we like it or not, life will teach us many things, unless we are incapable of learning. But there is needed a more active effort to bring up self and draw from it all its latent capabilities. Else our minds may lie fallow and our powers may rust. Of recent years there has sprung up quite a literature on what is called adult education, and endless books have been written on this theme—how to train the mind, to develop the memory, to strengthen the will, to acquire personality. Some of them are not without their value. I must leave the reader to study, if he thinks fit, such as may come to hand. ([1])

Meanwhile I trust that nothing here said will be taken as favouring mere selfish individualism to the tune of " I care for nobody, no not I, and nobody cares for me ", or " Every man for himself and the devil take the hindmost ", as though life were a perpetual scramble for what we want. Surely we can be true to our best selves while giving to others service, co-operation, kindness, and help, and gratefully receiving the like from them. The guarding and fostering of our individuality in no way conflicts either with man's nature as a social being or with the Divine Command, " Thou shalt love they neighbour *as thyself*". Nay, it is one of the paradoxes of Christianity that " individuality can be preserved only by sacrifice of individualism ".([2]) We are sent into this world with this supreme purpose—the worship of God and that first and foremost by the saving of our own souls. We might well concentrate all our efforts on that purpose. Yet the same Divine Master who said: " What doth it profit a man if he gain the whole world and suffer the loss of his own soul? " said also: " He that shall lose his life for my sake shall find it "—lose, that is, not merely his physical life by martyrdom, the lot of very few, but of his very self by self-denial, self-sacrifice, and self-forgetfulness: the Christian must " deny himself, take up his cross, and follow " Christ.([3]) Yet Christianity is the home, and is fast becoming the only home, of personality, the stronghold of the dignity of the human person, and the upholder of the true rights of man, no less than of his duties.

([1]) See next chapter and Appendix A.

([2]) R. H. Benson: *Paradoxes of Catholicism, p.* 109.

([3]) The doctrine of Christian self-denial is admirably set forth in *Learn of Me* by Father John Kearney, C.S.Sp. (Chapter V.)

CHAPTER III

ON MAKING THE MOST OF ONE'S SELF

THE very title of this chapter may surprise and disconcert some readers of ascetical literature. Had they not read in their spiritual books about self-denial, self-forgetfulness, self-sacrifice, nay even the annihilation of self? Have they not heard self-love denounced in the most uncompromising manner and the most unmeasured terms? Yet here is somebody about to tell us how to make the most of that outlaw, that miscreant self!

Well, dear reader, I am not going to contradict your revered spiritual writers. And yet I propose to begin this chapter by attempting no less a thing than the rehabilitation, the raising up out of the dust, of the love of self. And this, as shall presently be seen, is not a venture of audacious originality. For it has unexceptionable precedent and authority.

I

In the first place no less an authority than St. Thomas Aquinas teaches that there are three kinds of love of oneself, viz., first a love arising from our very nature and which, from a moral point of view, is neither bad nor good. Next there is a wrong kind of love which is of course blameworthy and which we have full liberty to denounce to our heart's content. But thirdly there is a love of self which springs from grace and is positively holy. How can this be? The answer is set forth at length by a disciple of St. Thomas and a member of his Order, Père Sertillanges, O.P.[1] I propose to follow his line of

[1] In a thoughtful and suggestive work entitled *Notre Vie*. (Paris: Revue des Jeunes, 1926).

26

thought, and then as best I may, to reinforce his conclusions. He boldly entitles his chapter " the virtuous
love of self ". And he argues thus—Are there not two
main reasons that lead us to love some thing or person,
viz., value or worthiness and nearness to ourselves. Now
for loving self we have these two reasons in a high
degree. As to the first, is not my ' self ' a human soul,
and so a child of God, God's workshop as it were, and
God's hope? Did He not create me, too, and fill me
with His love? Can I ignore all that and turn away
with loathing from my poor self? And as for nearness,
I may be *united* to others, but with myself I am actually
one. Again, what is it to love somebody? Is it not to
wish him good, his highest good? So to love myself is
to wish good to myself, it is to wish what God wishes,
to wish what God wants me to wish. If He wished me
merely to hate myself [1] why did He implant in me
that natural love of which St. Thomas speaks, that
instinctive love which includes the instinct of self-
preservation and much more besides.

To abandon interest in our own welfare, because we
hate and despise ourselves, would be to abandon the
task God has given us in this world, viz., to save at
least this one soul—our own. It would be to risk the
failure of one life, the frustration of one of God's hopes,
to bring about one of God's failures. This *ego*, this
soul of mine is, after all, a heavenly value, and not my
soul only but my body, too, since it is destined to share
my soul's eternal life.

Once more, we know, as was pointed out in our preceding chapter, that every soul is unique. It is evident
that it alone is fitted (and destined) to conduct its own
case, to follow it up in detail, to draw from itself all
that it can give. So that if every one were to abandon

---

[1] Yet Pascal could write, " La vraie et unique vertu est de se haïr (car
on est haïssable par la concupiscence) ". *Pensées*, ed Braunschvig. No. 485.
Pascal is often enough a dubious guide to thought and conduct.

self for the sake of others, each one's own providential rôle would be nullified, in no one would nature and supernature have its fulfilment, and so once more God's designs would be brought to naught.

This is but a part of the case made by our author for *l'amour vertueux de soi*. And surely it is conclusive, provided only that our love be of the right sort, a love united to God, ever falling in with and serving His holy will, and wishing for self the supreme goods of which the first and foremost is God's friendship. Indeed, as St. Bernard said, the highest point of love is to love one's self solely for the love of God.

To reinforce this argument by adding other authorities might well seem superfluous. Yet there may be those who think that the conclusion is merely one thinker's over-venturesome thought. Therefore I call next as witness Father Tilmann Pesch, S.J. In his work, *The Christian Philosophy of Life*, he has two chapters, the one entitled ' Justifiable Self-Love ', the other ' False Self-Love '. The latter is, of course, what all the ascetical writers denounce. Of the former he writes: " We are nowhere specially enjoined to esteem and love ourselves, seeing that this precept is clearly and legibly written in nature. Love for self, so Christ taught us, is to be the rule and measure of our love towards our neighbour. It is right that we should reverence ourselves [1] as being images of God, as being the work of His love and goodness, as being His property ". And he goes on to show how this love should be exercised in practice. Next, Dr. Cuthbert Hedley, O.S.B., in his *Retreat*, points out that the Christian is sometimes reproached with selfishness in living for the sake of heavenly happiness. But, he goes on, " there is no ' selfishness ' but only lawful self-solicitude in expecting and resolving to be finally happy."

---

[1] No writer on Christian morals would withhold a meed of praise from self-respect. Some of them even have a good word to say for self-reliance.

. . . " If this is ' selfishness ', it is of the very essence of nature and the most imperative command of grace ". Does not this " self-solicitude " arise out of well-ordered love?

No doubt this teaching is implicit in all Catholic ascetical writings. Yes, but it is seldom explicit. And in a chapter entitled ' Self Disparagement ' of his excellent little book, *Lift Up Your Hearts* (¹), Father Christopher Wilmot, S.J., dwells on the excesses of language, if not of thought, that are to be found in the writings of certain mystics especially in the sixteenth century. Such excesses, from which even the great St. Augustine was not free, are responsible, thinks our author, for many of the black and discouraging views that have obtained currency in the Church. And he appeals from these to the saner teaching of St. Thomas, St. Teresa of Avila, and most particularly St. Francis de Sales. St. Francis, in the *Introduction to the Devout Life*, has chapter after chapter with such headings as " Meditate on the Excellent Character of Thy Soul "; " On the Vast Stretch of its Intellect "; " On Thy Most Noble Power of Willing ", and so forth.(²)

II

We may then take it as a sound principle that there is a right and laudable love of self. It would seem to follow that we may, perhaps ought to, cultivate that self; and so self-education, self-culture, self-expression are laudable aims even from the highest point of view. The following passage from a work (³) of Dr. Edward Leen, C.S.Sp., may help to bring out this point:

(¹) London: Burns and Oates, 1949.

(²) In Appendix B will be found a number of passages, from authors of very varied types, each of them in praise of a right and laudable love of self.

(³) *The True Vine*, p. 212.

"Had man been created for a natural destiny
God would have assisted him to secure the fullest
measure of self-expression, using the word in its
rightful sense.([1]) When man has been created for
a supernatural destiny there is no reversal of God's
purpose. Supernatural elevation but opens up
indefinitely large possibilities of self-expression for
man. God made everything to be perfectly itself.
Man realizes God's purposes in his regard when he
achieves himself fully and expresses himself in the
supernatural order to the measure of his individual
capacity. Self-realization in and through grace is
God's will for man; and is the purpose of the whole
economy of his relations with man. Grace does not
eliminate, it but sublimates nature."

The question, then, remains to be considered, *How* to
achieve oneself fully, how so to develop oneself that one's
self-expression may be such as it ought to be. Were we
dealing with some product of man's industry and skill—
say a machine, we should say without hesitation that its
best, its only true, expression of itself is to work in the
way its makers designed it to work and meant that it
should work. Now God is the designer and as it were
the manufacturer of that marvellous machine, the human
being. It ought surely to find its truest expression in
working (i.e., acting) in the way it was designed to work
and in accordance with the nature given it. What *is* this
human nature; what is man; what is he meant to be
and to do? Tremendous questions! By false answers to
those questions given by false religions and false philo-
sophies millions of human beings have been led astray.
Though much in the nature of man remains obscure,
Christians, at all events, possess the answers to those

([1]) Unfortunately self-expression, in many books and articles to-day, is
taken to mean giving free rein to all our instincts and urges, in particular
our animal instincts. How false and pernicious such teaching is has been
set forth in a masterly way by Mgr. Fulton Sheen in his *Peace of Soul.* Ch. 9.

great questions. They know that man was created by God, that he is a compound of an animal and a spiritual element, that his body is not that of a beast, seeing that it is united with a spiritual element, or in other words, " informed by a rational soul ", that that rational soul is not a pure spirit, since it is united to, or rather compounded with, a material, animal element, the body. Within this human being there is a hierarchy of natures and of powers. His spiritual nature, whereby he is distinguished from the beasts, and its powers—his reason and rational will, must rule over and control his lower, animal nature.[1] All self-development, self-culture, must be based on these fundamental facts of human nature which to-day are assailed from many quarters, denied, and even derided. All self-development must take place within the framework of those truths. To ignore them is to court failure and even disaster.

But Christian man does not live merely on the natural plane. Being a Christian he must live the Christian life: he must follow the path traced out for him by Christ. If he follow faithfully this path he will go far towards making the most of himself and achieving self-development. Thus his lower nature will be subordinated to his higher by self-control and self-denial. The Christian virtues will enrich his personality. The service of Christ can call forth his best qualities and make them active in his life. The constant effort to curb his wayward desires and evil tendencies will teach him self-discipline. The Christian doctrine of the primal fall that has robbed his nature of immunity from evil and weakened its resistance to temptation will have taught him the need of this self-discipline. The Christian doctrine of repentance and forgiveness will drive sin from his soul and keep it from ruining his life. The Sacraments will nourish

---

[1] That is such functions of that nature as are under the control of the will. Many of them are, on the contrary, automatic.

his supernatural life, and prayer will keep him in touch with God. While the experience of his weakness and his falls might well have taught him self-distrust and a lowly notion of himself. Finally, as life goes on, he might well learn how different is this self-development and the endeavour to make the most of himself from selfishness, egotism, self-indulgence, self-absorption. All this supposes that the Christian lives his Christianity to the full. How many of us do?

III

Are we then to conclude that in the endeavour to make the most of ourselves all means other than the living of the Christian life are superfluous or impertinent? That conclusion, I think, would hardly be warranted. In the first place, what we may call supernatural means do not rule out the natural. God created the natural order as well as the supernatural. It is obvious, moreover, that certain skills and accomplishments *must* be acquired by natural means. Religion, to take a simple, everyday example, does not train the hands of the pianist or the typist. To go a little higher, it does not help to train the memory. And if these faculties are capable of training by natural means, why not also the mind and the will? These, no doubt, are spiritual faculties peculiar to man, yet they are closely bound up with his physical nature (brain, nerves, etc.) and can be reached and affected through that nature.

This training of the self and its powers ought to be begun and carried to a certain pitch in the course of what we call education. Such a statement may seem too obvious to be worth making. But, whatever about the theory of the educationists, in practice, education from primary to university too often amounts to mere instruction in a certain number of " subjects ". One feels sure that there are very many who, if this were said in their presence, would ask with surprise: ' Why, what else is it supposed to be?' I answer, with Mgr. Dupanloup, for I know no better definition of education—education is supposed to be: " The art of cultivating, exercising, developing, strengthening, refining all the faculties (physical, intellectual, moral, and religious) which go to make up in the child human nature [our contemporaries would say, ' personality '] and personal dignity; to give those faculties their destined perfection, thereby to train man to serve his country in the various social functions which he may be called upon to fulfil; and thus, aiming higher still, to prepare him for eternal life by means of the present life." (¹) A lofty ideal, certainly, and not easy of attainment in this workaday world. But surely worth aiming at. Another thoughtful writer on education (²) says that a boy or girl does not go to school to acquire a certain amount of book knowledge from the " three Rs " to philosophy and higher mathematics, but to be *trained for life*. And he goes on to point out four things not always mentioned in programmes and curricula but very necessary for life. They are (1) " A solid, rational, loving knowledge of his religion ". (2) The training of the character. (3) Catholic culture (" Our magnificent heritage of Catholic art and Catholic literature ") involving a training of the tastes, the feelings, and the appreciations, as well as of intellect, memory, and will. (4) A taste for worth-while reading.

But I am not presuming to attempt here, even in outline, a theory of education. If, however, education were always all that has been set forth above, I might end here this chapter on making the most of ourselves, for, our education completed, there would be little more that we could do towards self-achievement. Alas! in actual

(¹) *De l'Education*, Vol. I, p. 2. This is worked out in detail in *Le Caté-chisme de l'Education*.

(²) Father Edward Garesché, S.J.: *Training for Life*.

fact, education falls so far short of those ideals that young people are too often sent forth very ill-equipped for life.

I have still, therefore, to suggest as best I can, how, despite the shortcomings of one's formal education, one can nevertheless do something towards making the most of oneself. I shall point, then, first to the existence of a copious literature on personality and its achievement, and on the training of our faculties—mind or intellect, will, and memory. Books of this kind vary greatly in their nature and in their value. Some of them are built up on the basis of a false philosophy, and depend on erroneous ideas about human nature. But it would be a mistake to dismiss them all as the work at best of cranks and quacks. Many of them, on the contrary, contain helpful suggestions. Not a few are the work of sincere Christians and in particular of Catholic writers. One would do well to begin with these latter so as to be sure of one's ground. I shall name here a small number of them, leaving others to be mentioned in a longer list in an Appendix.

The first three are by French writers, but are to be had in English translations. Père Gratry's *Les Sources*, translated by the present writer under the title, *The Well-Springs*,([1]) was a very famous book in its day, and though now a little out of date in tone and presentation, is still a source of inspiration. It sets forth with a warm enthusiasm the way in which the thinker and the writer may secure the conditions in which the mind can work at its best and what are the qualities and dispositions, moral as well as intellectual, which are the best preparation for such mental work. A second book dealing with our mental life is *The Intellectual Life*, which has been translated from the French of the great Dominican writer, Père A. D. Sertillanges, O.P., by Professor Mary

---

([1]) London: Burns, Oates, 1931.

Ryan, and published by the Mercier Press, Cork. It is written primarily for what the French call "intellectuels", i.e., those who have chosen such careers as author, editor, professor, research worker, and the like, but much of it would be helpful to any educated person whose calling requires much brain work. It outlines the intellectual vocation, the virtues of a Catholic "intellectual", the organization of life, the time and field of work, the spirit of such work, etc., and makes many practical suggestions as to methods. Somewhat similar in scope and aim is the Abbé Dimnet's *The Art of Thinking*.(¹) It is more popular in presentation and enjoyed a great popular success in the United States.

Lastly, as far as mind-culture is concerned, I would recommend a book with the same title as Père Sertillanges, but very different in outlook and presentation—*The Intellectual Life*, by Philip Gilbert Hamerton. First published in 1873, it became a minor classic, and new editions were appearing well on into the twentieth century. It is full of vigorous thought, and is sound, on the whole, in outlook.

Personality, in its dictionary sense, is merely the abstract noun derived from person, as nationality is the abstract word derived from nation. In this sense, as I have already had occasion to remark, everybody has personality; one cannot be a person without having personality. But in books about personality the word seems always to imply some added adjective—a distinctive personality (strictly speaking all personality is distinctive, since no two persons are exactly alike), a distinguished, striking, strong, etc., etc., personality.(²) In this sense it is almost interchangeable with ' character '. The literature dealing with personality is very abundant, as will

---

(¹) London: Cape, 1931, New York: Simon and Schuster.

(²) Thus the author of *The Gain of Personality* mentions as the bases of it charm, force, sympathy, symmetry, optimism, and modesty.

be seen from the partial list in the Appendix. To that list, after the mention of a few outstanding books, I must refer the reader.

Personality and Successful Living (Milwaukee: Bruce, 1944) may be mentioned first. It is by Rev. James A. Magner, author of several able works such as *For God and Democracy*, and *Men of Mexico*, written from a definitely Catholic standpoint. The same may be said of *Personality: Its Formation and Action*, by William Healy (New York: Norton, 1938.)

On Being a Real Person, by Harry Emerson Fosdick (London: Student Christian Movement, 4th edition, 1946), is a thoughtful and suggestive book and Christian in outlook, with chapters such as " The Principle of Self-Acceptance ", " Using All There Is In Us ", " Mastering Depression ". It is a thoroughly helpful book.

It is important also that one should be aware of the comparatively new science of Psychiatry which professes to explain man to himself and enable him to cope better with the difficulties and emergencies of life. It is a sort of hygiene of our psychic powers, and there seems to be no reason to judge such hygiene useless or absurd. Mgr. Fulton Sheen writes: " In actual fact no moral theologian denies the validity and necessity of psychiatry."[1] But like any other science or mental discipline it can be pursued on wrong lines and diverted to unwarranted ends and purposes.

Fortunately those who wish to keep within Christian bounds have excellent guidance at their disposal. They need not become disciples of Freud and his psycho-analysis, nor of Coué and his auto-suggestion, nor of the Christian Scientists. They can avail themselves of what is true in these systems as well as of the writings of Jung, Adler, and so many others. But of recent years highly competent Catholic writers have entered this field.

[1] *Peace of Soul.* p. 195.

Mgr. Sheen's book, *Peace of Soul*,([1]) from which I have quoted the above judgment, is really a treatise on psychiatry, and much more besides. More recent still is *Psychiatry and Asceticism*, by Father Felix D. Duffy of the Congregation of the Holy Cross (St. Louis: Herder, 1950), a sound and balanced study of the relations between these two things. One of the foremost authorities is the Austrian Professor (now lecturing in America), Rudolf Allers, a critic of psycho-analysis, in his work, *The Successful Error*.([2]) His principal book on psychiatry is *Self-Improvement*, published in the U.S.A. by Benziger Bros., and in Ireland, but under the title, *Difficulties in Life*, by the Mercier Press (Cork), 1950. Another important authority is Dom Thomas Verner Moore, O.S.B., with his books on *Personal Mental Hygiene*, and on the *Driving Forces of Human Nature*.([3]) To these may be added *Safeguarding Mental Health*, by Raphael C. McCarthy, S.J.([4]) With such guides as these one is not likely to go far astray. In the preface to his *Difficulties in Life*, Dr. Allers says: " The arguments in the following pages are based on a definite philosophy. No treatise on human nature or any side of it can dispense with a philosophical basis. . . . This book is based on Christian philosophy and Christian morals."([5])

A book on the training of our various faculties with a view to our well-being and happiness is *Le Bonheur cet Inconnu* (Paris: Editions Spes, 1949), by Père Marcel-Marie Desmarais, O.P. Originally delivered as lectures to audiences of the general public, it is non-technical in

---

([1]) Published in Ireland by Browne and Nolan, 1950. The sales in the United States amounted to over 200,000 copies.

([2]) London: Sheed and Ward, 1941. See also his books on Character in the list appended to this chapter.

([3]) Both published in New York by Grune & Stratton, 1945 & 1948 respectively.

([4]) Milwaukee, Bruce, 1937.

([5]) There are copies of these books in the Catholic Library, Dublin.

style. After a preliminary chapter showing the reciprocal influence of the physical (man's animal nature) and the psychical (man's higher nature), he takes in turn each of our human faculties—imagination, emotions, memory, intellect, will, and shows how the training and use of each may affect our happiness.

As this book goes to press there has appeared a work on our present subject which would seem to be the best to date. It is *Psychiatry and Catholicism* by Father James H. Vander Veldt and Dr. Robert P. Odenwald. It is published by the McGraw-Hill Co. in the United States. The book first explains lucidly the meaning of personality, the moral law, conscience, responsibility, and then studies every variety of mental trouble, explaining modern methods of treatment and offering helpful and practical suggestions.

CHAPTER IV

ON THE DEFECTS OF ONE'S QUALITIES

IN Wilfrid Ward's *Life of Cardinal Wiseman* the author quotes Father John Morris's testimony to the Cardinal's " largeness of heart and broad sympathy which was always at work in him whenever and wherever it could find play. He had no anti-Irish, or anti-foreign, or anti-Jesuit, or anti-regular, or anti-convert, or anti-Old-Catholic feelings. It sufficed for him to be satisfied that anyone, or any body of people, or any cause, had a *bona fide* intention or tendency to do good, to obtain from him sanction or support or co-operation, as the case might be." All, I think, will admit that these were admirable qualities. But Father Morris goes on: " Of this and such-like qualities he may have had the concomitant defects: he was perhaps too merciful, too forgiving, too indulgent in the exercise of his high functions as an ecclesiastical superior."

To suffer from the defects of one's qualities is, as we shall presently point out, a token of the limitations of our human nature, limitations to which we may as well resign ourselves. But in the Cardinal's case it happened that these defects of his qualities led to much unhappiness, and might well have led to tragedy, were it not that the personalities involved were all good men and true, despite their shortcomings. For the Cardinal chose as his coadjutor, and as his private secretary, respectively, two men who possessed qualities in which he was utterly lacking, but who also suffered from the defects of those very qualities, and thereby caused the Cardinal to suffer also. The priest whom he chose as Coadjutor was Dr.

D

George Errington, a man of the utmost probity, conscientious in the discharge of all his duties, and strictly just. In this, no doubt, he did not differ from the Cardinal. But he was also a strict disciplinarian, enforcing rules and regulations with impartial severity, unbending and uncompromising. As he had, according to Father Morris, " little imagination and no pliability of will ", he saw straight before him and went ahead with " iron determination and persistency ". These were the defects of his qualities. Hence many painful clashes of temperament, leading in the end to complete estrangement.

On the other hand, Mgr. Searle, the Cardinal's life-long and devoted secretary, was, we are told, of the order of " rough diamonds ", a shrewd man of business and an accountant of almost exaggerated straightforwardness, whereas the Cardinal was like a child in regard to the management of money affairs. On the other hand, Mgr. Searle was " as narrow as he was honest ". He held the purse-strings and held them very tightly, in a way that was very galling to the Cardinal. Yet he " acted in good faith and in the confidence that he was faithfully serving the Cardinal, when in point of fact he was worrying him to death." He was also a man of fixed ideas, and when he took a dislike or distrust of anyone he held on to it for the rest of his days." Now it happened that the object of his most intense antipathy was one who, though totally different in character from the Cardinal, was Wiseman's right-hand man, so to speak, and destined to be his successor—Provost Henry Edward Manning, afterwards Cardinal. For this antipathy and determined opposition, which was fully concurred in by Dr. Errington, there were many motives, mistaken, no doubt, but not necessarily discreditable. For Dr. Manning, too, had certain defects of his qualities. At this time, as he humorously remarked later, he was still " a parson from the crown of his head to the soles of his feet." The unhappy consequences of the situation were strained relations, conflict, and estrangements. They might, as I have said, been much worse had not all the parties concerned been, at bottom, good and zealous men.

I have set forth at some length these particular examples of the defects of qualities—the shadows, as it were, of virtues, not as something untoward and exceptional, but as being, in this instance, striking in themselves and in their consequences. That it is not exceptional for qualities to be balanced not merely by defects but by the defects of those particular qualities, you may, I think, convince yourselves by a little thought about your experiences in life. You will have met somewhere among the byways the man who is businesslike, efficient, above all, practical—undoubted qualities, but who " has no use " for music, art, poetry, and other nonsense of that kind—an equally undoubted defect. You may also have met

> The man so various that he seemed to be
> Not one but all mankind's epitome . . .

the man who is interested in all sorts of things because his mind is open to everything that is good and beautiful. And you have probably noticed that he is all but useless in business and even in a profession, because what is needed there is narrow and almost exclusive concentration. His qualities of many-sided openness and wide sympathy have unfitted him for earning his living, at least along certain lines. No doubt you have fallen in with the good-natured, kindly, genial man, a good companion who brightens the dullness of the way, but—who cannot resist a drink, or any number of them. His best quality leads to his worst defect and to his undoing.

Indeed, the popular, generous-hearted man is too often prodigal and improvident: the prudent, cautious man is too circumspect to take risks, and the old adage is true here as elsewhere—" nothing venture, nothing win." Men who see all sides of a question are not only bad partisans but also incapable of throwing themselves wholeheartedly into any cause.([1]) A man who is a marvel of order and regularity is apt to fall into routine, rigidity, and woodenness. One who is modest and self-depreciatory may fail to make his own way in life and may prove a broken reed for all who lean upon him. G. K. Chesterton was almost an extreme case of the defects consequent on certain qualities. " For most people ", writes his biographer, " intensity of thought is much more difficult than action. With him it was the opposite. He used his mind unceasingly "—and to what splendid effect we know—" his body as little as possible." The result was that he became one of the most unpractical of men, " unpractical to a point almost inconceivable." And that again had this further consequence that for long (at least seven years in fact) after he was fully convinced of the truth of the Catholic Church, he still delayed entering it, for that of necessity meant the taking of a number of practical steps. Yet occasionally idealism and practicality are found combined in the same personality. His biographer writes as follows of Bishop Shanahan of Nigeria: " These two characteristics, system and vision, rarely co-exist in a human being. The man of system is generally the practical, hard-headed type, who can get far if he has drive and perseverance, and who can be a good administrator, if he has initiative and personality. The man of vision is normally something of an idealist, who sees things that others do not see, and at an elevation that others do not reach. He exalts, he ennobles, he uplifts. But he too often loses contact with the world around him and

---

([1]) " He had ", says a recent writer speaking of Cicero, " an over-fine perception of all the facts and facets of any situation, which palsied his power of action."

becomes a dreamer of dreams; or if he retains contact with the world, becomes disillusioned because of the gap between his high idealism and its crude realism. . . . Bishop Shanahan . . . was essentially and predominantly a man of vision. But there was too much practical energy and drive in his character to let him lose contact with his fellow-men, and too deep a fellow-feeling to allow him to forget how frail all humans are. . . . So he remained an idealist without ceasing to be a realist."[1]

I fancy it is true to say—but here your experience may not bear me out, that a man engaged in any all-absorbing profession is apt to pay for the qualities that win success in it, by certain shortcomings that it entails. Thus the Civil Servant, habituated to carrying out unquestioningly directions received from above, to hierarchical procedure, order, punctuality, is unlikely in later life to be a man of initiative and originality. He feels somewhat lost when orders cease to come down to him or cannot be passed on to subordinates. He is distressed by the haphazard ways of unofficial persons. It would be piquant to follow out this idea, applying it to other professions—to notice, for instance, how with medical men matters of bodily welfare may come to loom so large as to overshadow other interests and considerations. How the lawyer is apt to judge with the legal mind everything, however unrelated to the law. Perhaps you will call to mind some of Dickens's lawyers, Sergeant Buzfuz, or Mr. Striver, or Mr. Tulkinghorn, but of course some of those portraits were caricatures. Perhaps you have met somewhere in the byways ex-naval men like Captain Cuttle[2] or ex-military men like Major Bagstock, old Josh Bagstock, or like the notorious Colonel Blimp (largely created by the Leftist imagina-

---

[1] *Bishop Shanahan of Southern Nigeria.* By John P. Jordan, C.S.Sp. (Dublin: Clonmore & Reynolds). p. 215.

[2] " Captain Kettle " would be a more modern version, but even he no doubt is out of date.

tion). I must confess I have not hitherto encountered anybody much resembling these personages of fiction. Moreover, I wonder if your experience has been mine, that of meeting with men and women of every profession or calling who seem to have in but a slight degree, if at all, the defects of their professional qualities. Writers on the spiritual life are well aware of this infirmity of human nature. " One often has ", says one writer, " the defects opposed to one's good qualities. Firmness of character and a passion for exactitude will sometimes run to obstinacy, rigidness, and hardness towards others. Meekness is in danger of becoming weakness. Zeal may run us into criticism, impatience, anger. And so of the remainder."

" Many vices ", writes Father Maturin, " spring from virtues unbalanced by some other virtue which develops the opposite side of the character. One may, for instance, be all heart and no head or all head and no heart; if so, the powers, great and noble as they are, which belong to heart or head will fail of producing their proper fruit, for they are unbalanced and one-sided."

There must be a blending of the virtues. And he goes on to give examples:

" The virtue of Christian patience is the outcome of the perfect blending of gentleness (I should rather say meekness) and strength. If gentleness outweighs strength, patience degenerates into weakness; if strength outweighs gentleness it crystallises into hardness. Again, firmness is the blending, in perfect proportion, of strength of will and clearness of moral judgment; if there be not the latter, firmness will degenerate into obstinacy or scrupulosity; if strength of will be not in due proportion, then it is not firmness at all, but passes off into insincerity or even hypocrisy."

Father Faber, for his part, has among his *Spiritual Conferences* one entitled " Heaven and Hell ", in which he enlarges upon what he calls the eight diseases of the piety of his day.

As Père Charles, a Belgian Jesuit, writes: "God protects His work in us not only against our vices but also against our virtues or what we think are such." He goes on to show how easily these latter may be spoiled by the defects that may correspond to them. "You say, 'I want to avoid pride' and you fall into permanent idleness: 'I want to flee from ambition' and you take refuge in insignificance: 'I want to save my soul and so I have no time for my neighbour's': 'I am content to be pious, and don't bother to be useful.' After all, in order to live the devout life it really is not necessary to make ourselves unbearable to others, to dress like a scarecrow, keep away from all important activities, and drop half our work." . . . and much more to the same effect.

Next come to mind the differences in qualities and defects between the two sexes. That there are noteworthy differences not merely physical but temperamental between them is surely too plain to need proof, though there are those who speak and write as though these differences did not exist. 'Womanish' applied to a man and 'mannish' to a woman are both terms of disparagement. On the other hand we speak naturally of manliness, of manly strength and courage, of womanly sympathy and compassion, though neither sex is devoid either of courage or of sympathy. These differences do not mean that either sex is less gifted than the other. But each has its characteristic qualities which are not those of the other. When Tennyson wrote:

> Man for the field and woman for the hearth;
> Man for the sword and for the needle she;
> Man with the head and woman with the heart;
> Man to command and woman to obey.
> All else confusion

he was simplifying things overmuch. But in the third of these lines he touched upon what is, perhaps, the chief difference between man and woman—head and heart. Men, it is to be hoped, are not without heart, and women have often as good a head on their shoulders as any man. But with men it is commonly the head that leads, with woman the heart—the feelings and emotions. Now head and heart each in its place stand for precious qualities. Dickens describes one of his minor characters thus: " Polly Toodle was a good plain sample of a nature that is ever, in the mass, better, truer, higher, nobler, quicker to feel . . . all tenderness and piety, self-denial and self-devotion than the nature of men ". Dickens may seem to weigh the scales rather heavily on the feminine side of the balance. But let that pass.

These precious qualities, however, have, as we might expect, their corresponding defects. Men tend to rely wholly on cold logic and, as they will call it, common sense where it is not in place or not enough. Women think them hard and unfeeling. Moreover, making little of emotion in himself, a man is disconcerted, perhaps disgusted, to meet with it in others. So women often seem to him (and often are) temperamental, capricious, changeable (" La donna è mobile "). That is the seamy side of their best qualities. There are those verses of Sir Walter Scott, once so familiar as to be hackneyed—

> O woman! in our hours of ease
> Uncertain, coy, and hard to please,
> And variable as the shade
> By the light quivering aspen made;
> When pain and anguish wring the brow
> A ministering angel thou.

What is true of persons is often true of entire peoples. There is good in all of them—let that much be said against the racial fanatics and the ultra-nationalists. But the very qualities in which they excel may have their shadows, their resultant defects. Hear De Quincey on the English. Speaking of " those excesses to which energetic natures are liable through the very strength of their constitutional characteristics ", he writes:

" It is certain, for instance, that to the deep sincerity of British nature and to that shyness or principle of reserve which is inseparable from self-respect, must be traced philosophically the churlishness and unconciliatory bearing for which we are often and angrily arraigned by the smooth South of Europe." And he concludes: " Great faults therefore may grow out of great virtues in excess."

And here is G. K. Chesterton on the French:

" One might almost say that their vices are the flower of their virtues. Thus their obscenity (in literature) is the expression of their passionate love of dragging all things into the light. The avarice of their peasants means the independence of their peasants. What the English call their rudeness in the streets is a phase of their social equality. The worried look on their women is connected with the responsibility of their women. . . ."[1]

Somewhat paradoxical, it must be confessed, but then it is G.K.C.

And what of the Irish? That sincere patriot, William O'Brien, writes: " We, the Irish, are an imaginative race with all the inspiration but also the want of steadfastness appertaining to that quality." I must leave the reader to draw similar thumb-nail portraits of other nations.

Archbishop Ullathorne ventured to describe this fact of human nature at work in the religious orders. The passage in his autobiography is worthy of quotation, even if one may not quite agree with all he says:

" In studying the religious orders as spiritual schools, it has often occurred to me that while each has a characteristic temper and love of its own, and a disposition

[1] *All Things Considered*, p. 74.

to lean upon some individual quality or virtue as distinctive of its life and work, this very tendency requires a guard against its running into some correlative defect. And for want of this guard being always vigilantly observed Religious orders are mostly prone to deteriorate.

" Thus the temper of the Benedictine order is largeness of spirit or freedom, apt to degenerate into laxity. That of St. Francis is poverty, apt to degenerate into sordidness. That of St. Dominic is rigid law and science, apt to degenerate into the stiffness of the letter and pride of intellectual culture. That of St. Francis de Sales is spiritual sweetness, apt to degenerate into spiritual softness. That of the Carmelites contemplation, apt to degenerate into leaving Our Lord's Life and Passion in abeyance. That of the Jesuits is the practical, apt to discard the contemplative spirit and to degenerate into policy."[1]

The movements of thought or of action that have carried along with them great masses of mankind have had for the most part fine ideas and noble aims, but too often they were one-sided and unbalanced. The Renaissance could not have fascinated the *élite* of Europe had it not held up before the world an ideal of beauty and of perfection of form, but it embraced the paganism of classical antiquity along with its art, and so fell into moral corruption. The Catholic Counter-Reformation (I say nothing at the moment of the Protestant Reformation) was inspired by the glorious ideal of saving the Church of Christ from the assaults of heresy, but it engendered in the Church an attitude of controversy and defence from which we have scarcely even yet recovered. Nazism, perhaps, and certainly Italian Fascism, had ideals fine in themselves, but ideals that were blighted when leadership was perverted into totalitarianism. Classicism and

[1] Ullathorne: *From Cabin-boy to Archbishop*, p. 213.

romanticism each had its hours of glory, but each suffered from its counter-balancing defect which could have been offset only by the qualities of the other. That synthesis, blend, or balance was achieved only by the greatest. In lesser hands classicism became formal and cold and rigid—all intellect and no heart, while romanticism, with its cult of liberty and of sentiment, ran to seed in wild extravagance and sentimentality. One thoughtful writer[1] at least thinks that it could not have been otherwise, for the classical equilibrium (*ne quid nimis, in medio virtus*, and so forth), so desirable in itself, can be achieved only at the expense of other human values equally precious— heroism, enthusiasm, deep emotion, and the aspiration after greatness.

However that may be, it would seem that often a choice must be made between qualities: normally it is one *or* the other; one cannot have both. To be steadily consistent a man must be dispassionate and to some extent unimaginative, but men of that type forgo the grand power of arousing enthusiasm and stirring men to their depths. On the one hand you have the steady, judicious, reliable man, on the other the fiery genius or else the man of charm who can win over other men. Only in the very greatest men have these almost incompatible qualities been united.

Up to this point we may seem to have focussed our attention rather on the defects which are the shadows of our virtues than on the virtues themselves. But let us now assure ourselves that it is, after all, the virtues that really matter. It is incumbent on us, of course, to make every effort to rid ourselves of such defects as lead to the offence of God. But as for the others it is a mistake to be distressed about them, for they are often simply part of our make-up. It is best to remind ourselves that "to err is human" and that our Maker, too, is well

---

[1] Moeller: *Humanisme et Sainteté*.

aware of that and makes allowance for it, for " He knoweth our frame, He remembereth that we are dust."(¹)

Nay, we can go further and convince ourselves that these defects, yes even sinful faults, may come to have a value of their own for this life of ours. The very struggle against them is itself good for us. *Virtus in infirmitate perficitur,* strength is made perfect in infirmity "(²), i.e., by our very weakness and shortcomings, our struggles and failures. So that St. Paul could cry out paradoxically "when I am weak then I am strong." Better still, our defects may save us from conceit about our qualities, may even preserve us from the far worse vice of pride. " The web of our life is of a mingled yarn, good and ill together; our virtues would be proud if our faults whipped them not ", and, on the other hand, " our crimes would despair if they were not cherished by our virtues."(³) Here again we may call in the example of St. Paul. He wrote to his Corinthian converts: " Lest I should be lifted up overmuch by the grandeur of these revelations, there was given me a thorn in my flesh, an angel [? emissary] of Satan to buffet me."

G. K. Chesterton warns one in characteristic fashion not to pride oneself on one's qualities:

" A man will plume himself because he is not bad in some particular way when the truth is that he is not good enough to be bad in that particular way. Some priggish little clerk will say: ' I have reason to congratulate myself that I am a civilized person and not so bloodthirsty as the Mad Mullah '. Somebody ought to say to him: ' A really good man would be less bloodthirsty than the Mad Mullah, but you are less bloodthirsty, not because you are more of a good man, but because you are a great deal less of a man. You are less bloodthirsty

---

(¹) Ps. 102. 14.

(²) 2 Cor. XII. 9, 10. The whole passage, verses 7 to 10 should be read.

(³) *All's Well that Ends Well*, IV. 3.

not because you would spare your enemy but because you would run away from him." And he goes on presenting the counterpart of the point we are trying to make in this chapter: " Are we without the fault because we have the opposite virtue? Or, are we without the fault because we have the opposite fault? . . . Perhaps some great virtues have to be generated, as in men like Nelson or Emmet, before we can have certain vices at all, even as temptations."

Perhaps something like what we have just been saying is implied in these verses from *Measure for Measure:*

> " They say best men are moulded out of faults,
>   And for the most become much more the better
>   By being a little bad."

God knows how to draw good out of evil and to allow for all our shortcomings that are those of our human nature as He made it. And he repairs with such magnificence the damage wrought by the sins and wrongs of men that the Church, with holy daring, sings in Holy Week, *O felix culpa.* Why then should we repine because our petty qualities have their petty defects?

One man alone, and He was more than man, had *not* the defects of His qualities. As Archbishop Alban Goodier writes:

" Other men possess the weakness of their greatness; to be endowed with one high quality almost of necessity implies the lack of another; few men are two things at once, much less opposite things at once, none are at once perfect in every part. . . . Jesus Christ alone among men can be found wanting in nothing."[1] And therein He was unique.

---

[1] *Jesus Christ the Son of God,* p. 66.

CHAPTER V

TWO VIRTUES OF THE BYWAYS

As we travel through life, whether along the highways or through the byways, towards what our old handwriting copybooks used to call " that bourne from which no traveller returns ", we feel the need, or suffer from the absence, of certain qualities of mind and will. One of them is certainly courage, moral rather than physical, to stand up to the hindrances or break through the obstacles that beset our path. Another quality that ought to be combined with the last-named is persistence. For courage in moments of danger and difficulty is good, but in long periods of stress and perhaps of opposition it is not enough. Only persistence will carry one through. Persistence is not mere obstinacy, it is no mere butting blindly against stone walls. It is keeping right on despite obstruction in a path one knows to be right.

> To go on for ever and fail, and go on again
> And be mauled to the earth and arise,
> And contend for the shade of a word and a thing
>   not seen with the eyes;
> With the half of a broken hope for a pillow at night.
> That somehow the right is the right
> And the smooth shall bloom from the rough
> Lord, if that were enough. ([1])

It is fine, but hardly enough.

There is a humble and indeed duller virtue which is even more constantly needed in the byways of life than are those strong and virile qualities. I devote the first part of this chapter to it.

([1]) Robert Louis Stevenson.

1. PATIENCE

There is an old rhyme which begins

> Patience is a virtue
> Deny it if you can . . .

I forget the rest, but at all events that much of it expresses a truth: it is undeniable that patience *is* a virtue.([1]) It is not an attractive virtue: it looks at first sight too much like apathy, stolidity, mean-spiritedness. And is there not the variety of patience enshrined in the wicked old rhyme—

> Patience and persévérance
> Made a bishop of his Reverence.

But Christian patience is something very different. It will be worth our while to study its true nature.

It is clear, in the first place, that there are at least two kinds of patience. There is first the patience that connotes suffering (the Latin *pati* means to suffer). Endurance is almost a synonym of this kind of patience, and its opposite is complaining, murmuring, whining, self-pity, repining, rebelling, or simply breaking down and giving way. This is the patience of the martyrs under their physical sufferings, the patience of Job in his misfortunes, the patience of a patient (i.e., sufferer) in a hospital. It is also the patience of people who have sorrows and troubles and crosses of various kinds. You say of somebody: ' He has need of great patience: he has a great deal to put up with '. The prevalence of pain and sorrow in this life of ours is the measure of our need of patience.

The other kind of patience connotes not exactly suffering unless such as is involved in the passage of time without the accomplishment of something we have at heart or in our being thwarted in some way. Its

---

([1]) St. Thomas settles this point in the first article of the 136th question in his Secunda Secundae.

opposite is impatience, or losing patience. It consists in a kind of reining in of forces tending to fling off the incubus or obstructiveness of the thing under which we are said to be patient, restraining, for instance, " back answers " under rebuke, angry retort under criticism.

In this second sense one talks of unwearied or inexhaustible patience as though the passage of time wore down the resisting nerves. It is a kind of power of waiting without murmuring at having to do so. Thus God is said to be patient. He can afford to be patient, for He can afford to *wait*. Ought not we, all of us, feel deeply grateful for that Divine patience which puts up with our follies, forgetfulness, ingratitude, and sins, and yet forbears to strike. As Isaias says: " The Lord *waiteth* that He may have mercy on thee " (xxx. 18). Contrast the behaviour of the important people of the world. They do not know how to wait and they must not be kept waiting. Said Louis XIV, in his impatience, when some expected person pleaded his punctuality: ' *J'ai failli attendre* '—I was nearly having to wait.

Now what is to be our attitude in the various circumstances that try our patience? We might call in philosophy to our aid—a certain stoicism, or a touch of fatalism like the Moslem *kismet*, ' it is decreed '. We might repeat to ourselves the saying " What can't be cured must be endured ". We might, in short, make up our minds to " grin and bear it ".

But that, even for an ordinary Christian, is not good enough. For us Christians, suffering, sorrow, persecution, and the like, are not simply unmitigated evils. They are " crosses ", fragments of *His* cross. If we lived the full life of faith we should welcome them, embrace them. " My brethren ", wrote St. James to the early Christians, " count it all joy when you shall fall into divers trials, knowing that the trying of your faith worketh patience, and patience hath a perfect work ". And St. Paul kept repeating the same exhortation to joy in tribulation when writing to his much-tried neophytes.[1]

But I think it is not so much in the first kind of patience that we fail, at all events in the round of daily life: it is rather in the second. So let us look a little closer at the persons and things that try our patience in this way, the persons and things with regard to which it behoves us to keep patient. First come *ourselves*. There are those (and the writer is one of them) who, when they catch themselves doing or saying something of which their better selves disapprove, are wont to apostrophize themselves in opprobrious and insulting terms, ' You ass! ' being about the mildest term that seems to fit the case. It may be just a harmless way of ' blowing off steam ' or it may betray irritation and impatience. And this impatience may be due to annoyance that the very high opinion that we entertain about ourselves has received a setback. Again there is impatience, whether with our material defects and shortcomings or with our moral and spiritual faults and failings. I am afraid it is an outcome of wounded self-love. Sorrow and repentance, yes, that is all to the good, but impatience, No. It gets us nowhere. So with impatience arising out of the slowness of our progress in the spiritual life. It is quite out of place, to say the least. For, apart from moral miracles, all progress implies growth, and growth in all God's living nature is slow, even imperceptible. You don't see trees or babies grow. Spiritual growth may be far slower still and even more imperceptible. So let us not try any yard-sticks on our soul's stature nor set a time-limit to its growth.

Then there are our dealings with other persons. We all need a considerable fund of patience, for we live day in day out, often year in year out within a group

---

[1] For some references see the end of this Chapter.

E

of some kind whose members, however excellent, have their little peculiarities, and these may try one's patience as well as one's charity. But without confining ourselves to communal life, let us pass in review some types of persons who are liable to try one's patience. I need do little more than name them. There are of course the cranks or people whom we regard as such because their ways are not our ways. There are the difficult, the crotchety people, whom it is impossible to satisfy. There are the slow and stupid—they can't help it, but——. There are people of whom it is said that they do not easily suffer fools. Well they are just impatient people. There are the bores, well-meaning people, perhaps, but insufferably dull—or so they seem to certain others. There are the obstinate who refuse to give way or be persuaded. And there are the deaf. Some of these, as we say in Ireland, would without meaning it ' vex the patience of a saint '.

All these types may be found among our pupils if we are teachers, and among our penitents if we are priests. Now as regards teaching, well ' Education thy name is Patience ', and as for the confessional, if there be any virtue more needed there than patience I should be interested to hear of it. Impatience might mean a bad confession, or else the torture of scruples.

But ourselves and other people are not the only triers of our patience. Mere lifeless (or at all events irrational) things and circumstances can be very trying—weather that does not suit us, buses that do not arrive, bootlaces that break at the most awkward moments, cats that howl in the night, noises (doors that bang, windows that rattle, etc., etc.) which disturb us in the day-time, plans of ours that fail to work out, all that thwarts us in whatever way. To lose patience with these things may be less harmful than to lose it with persons, but it is even less reasonable, and it is quite useless. Which wise consideration, alas, has not hindered the writer from doing it often.

Yes, patience is certainly a virtue, but it ought not to be an isolated virtue. Without *humility* it is little better than stoicism. St. Paul says that *charity* is patient, no doubt because it knows how to make allowances and how to find excuses—for others. And St. Catherine of Siena says in her *Dialogue* that " love never goes alone, without her train of real virtues, and of these the principal is patience, which is the very marrow of love ". She also says that patience and *obedience* are inseparable. Again, since patience involves self-restraint, it is a form of self-denial and of *mortification*. When wrongs and calumnies, insults and affronts are patiently endured, patience may amount to heroism.

Finally, to be something more than a merely natural virtue, patience ought to spring from supernatural motives. There is the abiding thought of what we deserve to suffer because of our past. There is the thought of what we hope is coming to us. For " the sufferings of this life are not worthy to be compared with the glory that is to come " (Rom. VIII, 18). As the old song says, if I remember it rightly:

> Only a little way to stray
> Only a little way to roam
> Then safe at last, all danger past
> Safe in our Father's home.

Above all, there is the long-suffering patience of God. *Miserator et misericors Dominus, longanimis et multum misericors* (Ps. 102, 8), and the patience of Christ which shines forth from the Gospel narrative. If our inward eye were for ever fixed on the great Model, Christian patience would abide with us always.

*   *   *   *

This slight introduction to the study and cultivation of patience would have done its work if it could induce the reader to go further and read on patience—

St. Paul, Rom. v, 3; viii, 5; xv, 4; ix, 22; Cor. vi, 4; 2 Thess. iii, 5; 2 Tim. iv, 2 ; Hebr. x, 36.

The *Imitation of Christ*, Book III, chs. 16 to 19 (incl.) ending with a prayer to obtain patience.

St. Thomas, Summa 2a 2ae q. 136, and it would be worth one's while to read what Father Walter Farrell, O.P., so admirably writes about patience in his *Companion to the Summa*, Vol. III, pp. 393-5. Some good modern treatise on the virtues, such as those by Archbishop Ullathorne, Mgr. Gay, or Dr. Pearse of Maynooth.

2. CONTENTMENT

Contentment used to be one of the commonplaces of moral essayists and story-tellers. In our day it has taken on something of the nature of a burning question. For religion, because it commends contentment, has been arraigned as being the opium of the people, a mere narcotic numbing all endeavour and all aspiration after better things. The charge is false, but it is certainly specious, and if we Christians are to rebut it and to convince the masses that there is no real substance in it, we ought surely make our minds clear as to what is involved in this notion of contentment. Is it a good thing or an evil thing? Does it make for happiness or hinder its attainment? Is it a virtue or a vice?

Contentment seems to me a sort of equilibrium between possession and desire, between having and wanting. According as the balance leans to the side of possession or to the side of desire a man is more satisfied or less. But note that to be less satisfied, to be unsatisfied, even, is not to be discontented. It is only when equilibrium is lost and the scale of the balance comes down heavily on the side of desire that you have the discontented man, not to say the malcontent. And on the other hand, when the scale comes down heavily on the side of possession, you have mere smug self-satisfaction or passive and supine acceptance of things as they are. Thus, contentment has this in common with the virtues, that it is a difficult middle way between two extremes. It does not stifle desire and aspiration, yet will not allow itself to be swept helplessly onward by tyrannous, insatiable desires and Utopian aspirations. It is a certain provisional acceptance of the present without acceptance of a future that is likely to be no better. It rests in what it has, while reaching out to better things as yet beyond its grasp.

The idealist and the saint (always an idealist after his own fashion) is never wholly satisfied, because the ideal is by its very definition some high object of endeavour which inspires and draws a man towards it and to which he may ever approximate (as asymptote to curve ([1])) without ever fully attaining it. He values what he has, he does not despise the present, but he is allured by visions of a better future, he is stirred by aspirations after higher things. This is that " divine discontent " of which we sometimes hear. Clearly it is something very different from the mere discontentedness of the disgruntled or from that unrest of which likewise we hear so much. There may indeed be causes, only too real, of discontent and unrest. What for the moment I am contending is that unrest and discontent are a frame of mind very different from the unceasing urge and the unending quest of the idealist and the saint.([2])

If ever man felt within him that " divine discontent " it was St. Paul the Apostle. He was the most unsatisfied of men, never resting, ever moving on to fresh conquests for the Christ who had struck him down on the Damascus road, until at last the Roman empire laid a chain upon

---

([1]) This geometrical illustration is Father Joseph Rickaby's.

([2]) " The only dreadful thing in life ", said Father Bede Jarrett in this spirit, " is to be content with life."

him and held him fast till he was ripe for martyrdom. Yet it is precisely St. Paul who is the great preacher of contentment. He himself would seem to have attained it not without a struggle. " I have *learned* ", he wrote to the Philippians, " in whatever state I am to be content therewith ", yes, content even at the moment when he was setting out for as yet untrodden lands and as yet unforeseen labours and trials. And as he was himself, he would have others be—" Be nothing solicitous ", he wrote to those same Philippians. To his disciple Timothy he wrote: " Godliness with contentment is great gain. For we brought nothing into the world, neither can we take anything away; but having food and clothing, with these we shall be content." And there is a similar phrase in Hebrews: " Let your way of life be without covetousness, contented with such things as you have."

We may recall here all that in the New Testament is said of peace, for peace and contentment are kindred frames of mind. The most casual reader of the Gospels could hardly fail to notice the value set on peace, from the angels' song at Bethlehem—" Peace on earth to men of good will "—to the Saviour's parting words in the Supper Room—" My peace I leave you, My peace I give unto you, not as the world gives do I give unto you." St. Paul, faithfully interpreting the Master, speaks at one time of " the peace of God which surpasseth all understanding " and prays that it may take possession of the hearts of his converts, at another of the " peace of Christ " which is to fill with joy the hearts of the Christians of Colossae, *Gratia et pax* was the typical greeting of the early Church, echoed in the " *pax vobiscum* " of our liturgy.[1] Can there be any true inward peace without contentment?

---

[1] Phil. vi. 7; Col. iii. 16. Cf. Romans ii. 10, and xiv, 17.
Note that the first of the three prayers said by the priest just before his Communion is a prayer for peace.

Contentment, then, would seem to be a frame of mind in harmony with the Christian spirit and prized by the founders of Christianity.

On the other hand, we have seen, there is the " divine discontent " of the idealist and the saint and that, too, would seem to be in harmony with the Christian spirit. Indeed Christianity teaches and fosters this divine discontent, for it keeps ever reminding us in St. Paul's phrase that " we have not here a lasting city but look for one that is to come." We are in this world as pilgrims and sojourners, ever aware that nowhere in it is to be found our heaven and final home.

It is just here that Christianity comes into inevitable conflict with all those for whom there is nothing beyond the horizon of this world. For if Christians look for their true home and heaven to a life beyond the grave, the atheist, the materialist, above all the Communist, wants it here and now. If the Christian outlook is to influence life, if the Christian faith and hope is to flow into conduct, then life in this world, not individual life only, but social and national life, must be ordered in view of the life to come. The Christian faith in the hereafter ought to work out into a technique for the life here below wholly different from that of the life which does not look beyond the grave, but dreams that

> " Earth can be the Paradise
> It never was to human eyes
> Since our first sun arose and set."

We know, alas, how many professing Christians live as though the life to come were but a pious tale or some " far off divine event " which had little to do with their daily lives. With such the Communist should have no quarrel, for in practice their outlook differs little from his own. With them, contentment, where it exists, is hardly a virtue.

Still less is it a virtue with such as, like those in the Gospel against whom Christ pronounced woe, " have peace in their possessions ", and are so wholly absorbed in business and money, in getting and spending, that they have no thought to spare either for higher things or for their less fortunate or weaker or downtrodden brethren in that humanity of which they form a part; or with such as the Pharisee who thanked God and himself for his virtues and his prosperity. There is a type of well-to-do, comfortable, self-complacent middle class people who are of the world worldly, and whose contentment is a mere caricature of true Christian contentment. And, though they are far from representing their class as it really is to-day (for the best of the middle class have fallen on evil days), these are taken by the proletarian or left-wing writer as typical, and held up to the scorn and execration of the masses.

But the Communist feels no grievance about the contentment of the bourgeoisie. For him the bourgeoisie is past redemption and must simply be " liquidated ". What enrages him is contentment among the " proletariat ", for, as it seems to him, contentment paralyzes it, rendering it impotent in that class war which is his principal weapon for the attainment of his aims. And so he hates and scorns contentment as he hates and scorns the other Christian virtues—charity, meekness, chastity, " mercy, benignity, humility, modesty, patience " (Colossians III, 9-12). These are the Communist *vices*.[1]

And now we are face to face with the real issue: Does contentment, in common with its sister virtues, patience, submission to authority, meekness and the like, incapacitate the people of the byways in their struggle to better their lot, or rather would it do so if the practice of these virtues were general among men? [2]

---

[1] Hardly less were they vices in the German National-Socialist Ideology.

[2] This is perhaps the place to call attention to an excellent study en-

Before replying directly let me deal with what may seem, in comparison, a minor question. The Communist —let him deny it how he will—has one pursuit in common with the rest of us, upper class, bourgeois, or of no class at all, and that is happiness. Now, does contentment make for happiness? and, on the other hand, is perpetual discontent compatible with happiness? The right answer to both questions is manifest. Mankind, I think it may be said, has ever held contentment to be indispensable to happiness. Its verdict might be summed up in the verse of an English humorist:

> " Let this plain truth those ingrates strike
> Who still, though blessed, new blessings crave,
> That we may all have what we like
> Simply by liking what we have."

Thus contentment takes to some extent the place of possessions and gives us such happiness as we might draw from them. Even a pagan poet like Horace often dwells on this theme:

> " Non possidentem multa vocaveris Recte beatum . . ."
> 　　　　　　　　　　　(*Odes. IV. 9.*)

or

> 　　　　　　　　" multa petentibus
> Desunt multa: bene est cui Deus obtulit
> 　　Parca quod satis est manu."
> 　　　　　　　　　　　(*Odes.* III. 16.) [1]

But it is enough to recall one's own experience of life. Has not contentment been possible with very much less than we might desire and has not happiness followed upon contentment?

titled " Religion—Drug or Cure? ", contributed by the late Father J. E. Canavan, S.J., to the *Irish Monthly*, January, February, March, 1935.

[1] You would be right in calling the man of few possessions a happy man. Again—Those who are looking for many things feel the lack of many things: it is well with the man to whom God with sparing hand has given just enough.

But the Communist would probably answer our questions by saying, " Yes, discontent destroys happiness for the time, but only to ensure it at some future date for some future generation when the struggle of the proletariat shall have issued in triumph ". It sounds heroic, self-sacrificing, and undoubtedly there have been visionaries and fanatics who have sacrificed their all for this proletarian Utopia. But what of the people of the byways? What, gentle reader, about you and me? Surely life is too short to put off one's happiness, such as it is, to an indefinite future time when all that will be left of us (so the Communist believes) will be a little ashes or a little clay. Christians seek some measure of happiness even here below, while hoping and longing for the immeasurable and unending happiness which awaits them beyond the grave.

But let us return to the question of contentment and its effect upon the " class struggle ". The position of the believing Catholic is in the first place this—" If conscience impedes me, if the practice of Christianity or of any Christian virtues handicaps me in the class struggle, why then so much the worse for the class struggle: I am a Christian first and foremost. If your struggle for what you call the emancipation of the masses involves what Christian morality characterizes as murder, lying, fraud, oath-bound conspiracy, or the like, then you must do without me. A triumph won at the cost of my soul and its immortal destiny would be not gain, but utter loss. But if you ask me to throw myself into the struggle for justice and fair play and human living conditions and security for the future on my own behalf and that of my fellow-toilers, I am with you heart and soul, even if need be to the use of the dangerous weapon of the strike. My Christianity does not hinder me in that but rather urges me on." And in point of fact the Christian Trades Unionist, the Catholic working-man fights as strenuously for the rights of labour as the working-man who has abandoned Christianity. But I am only too well aware that for the thorough-going Communist, and even the socialist, such protests and assurances are but idle breath. They have convinced themselves that *all* means are good that lead to social revolution, and perhaps the most violent means are the most effective. 'If foul (¹) means may be used, it is but foolishness to try fair means first; let us begin with the foul and the struggle will be the sooner ended'. Here Christianity cries halt, and therein lies the real grievance against it. It is not an opiate that numbs: it is a cordial that stimulates to action, but only within the limits of the law of God.

But, it may still be argued, what of your " conformity with the will of God ? "; what of your humility?; for these, you will admit, are the real bases of contentedness. Do not these make for unprogressive inertia and acceptance of things as they are? For the former seems to say: " All that is willed by God is best for us, and all things that are, are willed by God. Therefore what is, is best. Let us accept it without looking beyond." And humility: " I do not deserve any better than what I have. Therefore let me be content with it and look for nothing more." It would not be hard to point out the fallacies in such a statement of the case. But let us take it in a different way. The Christian belief in Providence and the Fatherhood of God is something essentially other than Oriental fatalism. Christians know that God in His ordinary Providence expects them to use to the best purpose the powers and faculties and talents that He has given them. Hence the traditional and accepted adages: " God helps those who help themselves ", " God who has made man without himself will not save him without himself ", " Pray as though everything

---

(¹) Foul, that is to say, from the point of view of Christian ethics.

depended on God's help and act as though everything depended on yourself". Cromwell's "Trust God and keep your powder dry" is in the same tradition, though one might be somewhat dubious about the spirit of it. No, a Catholic's temperament and personal limitations may handicap him in the fight for justice and for better things. His religion will be no hindrance.

Then again the Church and Catholic tradition has always distinguished in Christ's teaching *precepts* or commands binding under sin and *counsels* which are, what the name implies, pieces of advice, of divine advice indeed, lofty ideals of moral conduct to which the Christian is invited to rise if he is able. *Qui potest capere capiat*, said Our Lord.

But in all this a still wider question seems to be involved. The prejudice that Christian contentment, with its kindred virtues, implies mere self-satisfaction, inertia, indifference to the progress of the world and the forward struggle of mankind, is one by no means peculiar to Communists. It is widespread, and seems to me to account for much of the prevailing prejudice against the Church. The Christian is bidden to be contented with his lot, to be detached from the world, to be unworldly. So it would appear that this world is of no consequence whatsoever and this life of ours a vain thing. Do not certain writers of the Bible exhaust metaphor in describing its nothingness? it is a shadow, a mist, a flower that fades in a night, a dream, an arrow cleaving the air and leaving no trace behind. Yes, but we must not forget a distinction which Christians feel in their bones even if they fail to formulate it. It is this: that taken in and by itself, bereft of the significance which Christian faith gives to it, life *is* a vain and empty thing, and how many thousands of human beings have found and felt it to be so.

But seen in the light of Christian faith, *sub specie æternitatis*, it is a great and noble and significant thing, inasmuch as it is our time of trial and preparation for eternity. After all, how is it possible that this world could be of no consequence, seeing that God made it and maintains it? How is it possible that this life should be of no consequence, seeing that Christ lived it and wills that countless millions of mankind should live it? If the world be worthless, why should it be at all? If life be meaningless, why are human beings created to live it?

It is the purpose of the Church to help men so to use the world and life that they may gain eternity. If she is ever insisting on the paramount importance of the life to come, it is not that she despises the life of this world, but that she knows how prone men are to forget the other.

And so, if she preaches patience amid the troubles and sufferings of this life and contentment with the measure of present good and joy life has to offer, it is not because she wishes us to rest satisfied and stagnant at any stage of the onward march of time, or to stifle all longings for better things hereafter and even here below.([1]) There is no virtue in merely vegetating even in the byways of life. Far from it. It is because patience and contentment are in themselves good things and make for that modicum of happiness without which it is hard for men to live their lives and work out their salvation. These virtues are no obstacle to the progress of mankind nor even to the economic development of the world.

Moreover, Christianity has always taught that man is a social being. He is not meant to stand alone. He has manifold duties towards his fellows, and the Church has

---

([1]) The following sentence is from the Right Rev. Ottokar Prohaszka's *Meditations on the Gospels* (Sheed & Ward, 1937), Vol. I., p. 128: " Let us avoid everything that paralyzes human endeavour and replaces it by slavish inertia, and all that numbs enthusiasm and leads to tame resignation."

a social doctrine which he may not ignore, in so far as it concerns him. He must not immure himself in any little walled garden of selfish contentment, or rather self-satisfaction, and oblivious peace. No doubt there have been and are solitaries, anchorites, recluses. But these by their prayer and penance and the high example of their lives give to their fellow-men that service which others render by active co-operation.

Finally, to hold that there are values far higher than the material and economic is not to contemn nor even undervalue these latter; it is to put first things first. To say that not by bread alone doth man live is not to cast aspersions on our daily food; it is to recognize the hierarchy of things. And this is after all but common sense. It can be folly only to those who deny the spiritual and the supernatural altogether.

There is, then, I submit, no reason why men who profess to be Christians should not cultivate contentment. There are solid reasons why they should. If we of the byways be wise we shall, like St. Paul, " learn to be content."

Some sage has advised the man who cannot get what he likes to try liking what he gets. Good advice, but not so simple as it sounds. It is, perhaps more helpful to say—and thereby to sum up what I have been trying to bring out in this chapter—that it is only human to be unsatisfied with one's material lot, that it is even praiseworthy to be ever unsatisfied intellectually and spiritually, but that to be dissatisfied, discontented, disgruntled, is to be one's own worst enemy.

CHAPTER VI

FELLOW-WAYFARERS

WERE we in literal reality to frequent the main roads and the by-roads, the towns and the villages, we should no doubt in the course of a life-time fall in with all sorts and conditions of men. As things are, that is likely to be the fortune or misfortune only of tramps and gipsies. Most of us are much more restricted as to the variety of our acquaintances. The barriers of class, group, profession, the narrow range of our movements, these and other circumstances hem us in and greatly restrict our contacts.

But though we do not come into contact with all sorts and conditions of men, there are certain types which, as the years go by, we cannot fail to meet. Did space and the reader's patience permit, it would be amusing to attempt, as La Bruyère in his *Les Caractères* attempted, pen portraits of all of these. I do not feel equal to the task. Rather shall I choose, somewhat arbitrarily, two or three only, perhaps with passing allusions to some others.

1. THE CYNIC

Do dogs sneer? I cannot say. But if they do, certain it is that the poor things do not know they are doing it. So is it not an unjust reflection on the canine race that the word cynicism should be formed from the Greek word for a dog?

There was, as we know, a school of philosophers in ancient Greece who chose to model their manners on the less admirable aspects of doggish character, its roughness and aggressiveness. Men nicknamed them cynics in disdainful allusion to their ways, but they, far from taking umbrage, adopted the dog as their badge and symbol. So at least we are told.

But the traits of doggish nature do not suffice to describe the cynic as we know him to-day. He demands a more searching characterisation and deserves it. Let us see what can be said about him.

The root characteristic of his temperament is that he has no belief in, no respect for, human nature. He may go further and believe that human nature is rotten at the core. He believes that he sees through all the seeming virtues of his fellow-men; and has his own definitions for them—gratitude? a lively expectation of favours to come. Humility? when it is not mean-spirited crawling is a dexterous way of extracting praise from others. Religion? Dope for dupes and *naifs* and a money-making business for those who run it. Patriotism? Mostly a loud-voiced advocacy of the winning side in politics.([1]) Charity? the pleasure of seeing your name high up on subscription lists. Love? another name for lust, or else just self-love in disguise. And so with many of men's activities: politics—nothing but graft, bribery, and a scramble for the spoils of office; education—a throwing of artificial pearls before real swine.

Whatever the apparent excellence of the actions of those around him, he is unimpressed. He has his doubts about their *motives;* for he discounts disinterestedness and is frankly sceptical of sincerity. *He* is not going to take people at their face value.

As for value, somebody has unkindly said of the cynic that he knows the price of everything and of everyone and the value of nothing. He probably would pride

---

([1]) Old Samuel Johnson once described patriotism as the last refuge of a scoundrel. But Johnson was no cynic. He had in mind certain politicians of his day.

himself on his discernment in detecting the absence of value in men and things. *He* at least has no illusions, while for the generous illusions and enthusiasms of youth he has nothing but contempt.

In short, the cynic neither trusts nor hopes nor loves.

Unfortunately for him, other people seem unable to admire these characteristics of his. Many of them would agree with Tennyson (as reported by Wilfrid Ward in *Problems and Persons*) that cynicism is a sign of intellectual shallowness and littleness. Simply to despise, he insisted, means nearly always not to understand. The narrow-minded despise what is beyond their ken. People who live always in a little coterie look down on all outside. And Tennyson quotes with admiration these lines of another poet, Wordsworth:

> Stranger henceforth be warned and learn that pride
> Howe'er disguised in his own majesty
> Is littleness, that he who feels contempt
> For any living thing hath faculties
> Which he has never used; that thought with him
> Is in its infancy . . .

Others, too, seem to agree with Wordsworth that somewhere at the back of cynicism there is conceit and possibly a wounded egotism.

But the reason for such conceit is hard indeed to discover, for, truth to tell, cynicism, like ' strong ' language, is an outcome of weakness; it connotes an incapacity. It is the bitter froth of a shallow mind, encased, as often as not, in a weakling frame—the very antithesis of *mens sana in corpore sano*.([1]) It is a mind that has never peered deep enough into life to become aware of its real seriousness, a mind that has not probed the human heart enough to know that, if it is capable of hideous wickedness and meanness, it is also capable of self-

---

([1]) A healthy mind in a healthy body.

F

sacrifice and love, of nobleness and generosity, of endurance and bravery even to heroism.

If there be one thing more than another on which the cynic prides himself it is that he never gives way to foolish admiration of anything or anybody. Here is what the famous Dr. Arnold of Rugby wrote about that aspect of the cynic's personality:

" I believe that *nil admirari* is the devil's favourite text, and he could not choose a better to introduce his pupils into the more esoteric parts of his doctrine. And therefore I have always looked upon a man infected with this disorder of anti-romance as one who has lost the finest part of his nature and his best protection against everything low and foolish."

Another writes:

" We need not fear those who look us through and through so much as those who look just beneath the fair-seeming surface. This last is the half-penetration which breeds cynicism in him who knows little of God, little of himself, and therefore little of his fellow-men. The Christian cynic is a square circle."

' Oh come now ', somebody will say, ' this is a little too much. The cynics we have known are not so bad as that '. And he is probably right. Few indeed are those in actual fact who are cynics through and through, who are nothing if not cynics. Nay more, if there is nothing whatever to be said for cynicism, there may be something to be said for cynics.

It is no defence of them to plead that their cynicism is a source of satisfaction, to feel that at any rate *they* are not to be taken in, not to be hoodwinked by fair words or by pseudo virtues, that they cannot be disappointed in men because they never had any hopes of them, to feel the peculiar pleasure of pondering in their minds ' What dupes, what fools men are! ' That plea cannot be admitted, for it is a plea for cynicism itself.

But very often cynicism is merely a *pose;* a man is a cynic only from the lips outward. To put it another way his cynicism may be only skin-deep. Or else cynicism may be a mask to hide real, and it may be, deeply wounded feelings or the first bitterness left by some shattered illusion. Yet even cynicism such as that does evil work in other minds. To corrode with sneers is worse than to " damn with faint praise ".

Indeed, as no man is born a cynic, if a man becomes one, it may be that it is his experiences in life that have made him so, and there are experiences in life that drive a man to the verge of cynicism, experiences that wring from him such bitter cries as ' inconstancy thy name is woman ', or, as the Psalmist of old " said in his excess ", ' Every man is a liar ', such cries as might be forced from the lips of a King Lear, a Timon of Athens, or an Othello, in the depths of their bitter disillusionment.

In the grip of such experiences a man may for the moment lose faith in man; he may for the moment cease to believe that there is honour or honesty, gratitude or faithfulness anywhere to be found. But in soberer mood, or when the cloud has passed away, he will pull himself together and revive his faith in his fellow-wayfarers.

Then, besides those who for a time lapse into a cynicism which is alien to their true nature, there are those who are often mistaken for cynics. The pessimist may be wrong in taking the gloomy view, but he is not thereby a cynic. Ecclesiastes, with his melancholy refrain, ' Vanity of vanities and all is vanity ' was not a cynic. The satirist may be harsh and bitter and even savage in his scourging of vice and folly. But neither is he thereby a cynic. Nor are denouncers, however violent, of injustice and of wrong, the Langlands, the Savonarolas, the Leon Bloys.

The frames of mind just mentioned are certainly not the same as cynicism. But neither are they its antithesis. We need not seek among them for an antidote to cynicism. If we would exorcise the spirit of cynicism, we must, I think, call in other spirits to drive it out. And these other spirits, I suggest, are the spirit of little children, the spirit of the poets, and the spirit of heroes and saints.

Christ held up childhood before Christians as a model for their lives: " Unless ye become as little children ye shall not enter the Kingdom of Heaven." He did not wish us to remain children always; He would have us keep all we can of what is precious in childhood. And what does it mean to be a child? For an answer I might quote Fathers of the Church and many a Christian writer down the ages. Instead, I shall merely cite a sentence or two from Francis Thompson: " What is it to be a child? . . . It is to have a spirit yet streaming from the waters of baptism; it is to believe in love, to believe in loveliness, to believe in belief." Those few words sum up the beauty of spiritual childhood in contrast with the ugliness of cynicism.

As to the poets—I have been trying to think of any great poet who was also a cynic—Homer, Pindar, Virgil, Horace, Dante, Chaucer, Tasso, Camoens, Ronsard, Calderon, Shakespeare, Milton, Corneille, Racine, Dryden, Pope, Goethe, the Lake Poets, Shelley, Keats, Byron—ah, Byron, you say: What of *Don Juan?* Well, but it is hard to say which is the true Byron, the romantic, poetic Byron of *Childe Harold* and so much besides, or the cynical, sneering Byron of *Don Juan.* Anyhow he is, so far, clearly an exception, and an exception that seems to prove the rule. For we can continue the litany even to our own days—Tennyson, Arnold, Browning, Longfellow, Lamartine, Swinburne (yes, even Swinburne), Hopkins, Thompson, Bridges, Noyes, Claudel. Who would call any of these a cynic? (¹) If we are in search of cynics we could find them only among the minor decadents. But I think that in the *Golden Treasury* and the *Oxford Book of English Verse*, for all their comprehensiveness, you will hardly find a note of real cynicism. For poetry, as distinct from light verse, moves in an atmosphere of the ideal. Of its very nature it is lifted up above the level of prose; it is the outcome of a mood of emotional and imaginative exaltation, whereas cynicism is a mood of emotional depression and a sort of atrophy of the imagination. It despises love and enthusiasm and eager hopes: it is without faith and truth. The poetic spirit means with Tennyson " the love of love, the scorn of scorn, the hate of hate." So much for the poets.

Above all there are the heroes, authentic, historical. Not the supermen of German dreamers. But men often humble and obscure who by their very lives and deaths give the lie to the cynic and to all who have despaired of the human race. There is the courage, the endurance, the indomitable perseverance of the Arctic explorers. There is the reckless daring or unflinching steadfastness in the face of death of millions of common soldiers in every war that was ever fought, and not least in the last of them. There has been all down the stream of history selfless devotedness to many a cause good and bad.

Rising still higher than these heroisms there is the heroism of the Saints, heroes of holiness. And if holiness be, as no doubt it is, a word without meaning to the cynic, there are still the martyrs. To suffer torture and death for one's convictions—*that* they might well accept as a fact, even if they do not understand it. And the historical martyrs of Christianity are counted by the hundred thousand—rich men and slaves, old men and young, women and young girls, men and women of every race all down the ages.

___

(¹) Who would associate cynicism with Crashaw, Goldsmith, Gray, Blake, Scott, Burns, Moore, Mangan, Ferguson, Davis?

No, there are, no doubt, the seeds of evil in all of us, but all men are not, as the cynic would have them to be, humbugs, hypocrites, or knaves in the last analysis. We need not even study the heroes to be sure of that. There is still in the world, as there has always been, that beautiful thing, a mother's love. There is the faithful if unromantic love of the Darbys and Joans of the world, lasting through weal and woe, unto grey hairs and even to the grave. There is lifelong devotion to an ideal. There is gratitude that is genuine and affection that is unselfish, and patience and humble resignation, even outside the bounds of sainthood. If the cynic does not know these things, it is because he does not know life or is incapable of interpreting it.

And the moral of all this is that for us of the byways the cynic is not a desirable fellow-wayfarer. Nay, it were best for our happiness and peace of mind to eschew his company altogether.

2. THE PESSIMIST

The pessimist is a very different type of person from the cynic. He does not sneer; he merely groans and sighs. Like Tennyson's doves he " makes perpetual moan ". I have known one cheerful pessimist who kept ever smilingly foreboding ruin and disaster. But usually the brow of the pessimist is wrinkled, his eye lack-lustre, and the corners of his mouth turned downwards. If he smiles at all, it is a bitter smile that greets the foolish optimism of the man who ventures to say that things are going pretty well. The seamy side of life is his chosen domain, and that is no laughing matter. If you meet him in the byways do not linger with him, for his pessimism is infectious.

It is true that there are various species of pessimists, some more and some less desirable as fellow-travellers.

There is, for instance, the *laudator temporis acti*, the man for whom everything good and beautiful belongs to the past and who has no good word for the present. He is ever talking about the good old days and contrasting them with the times he is living in now. It is only fair to admit that this nostalgia is natural enough in many people—the elderly sportsman who entertains us with tales of his prowess at cricket or football in his young days or with his past exploits in the hunting field; the ageing mother who sits dreaming of the days when her children were children and filled the home with happy laughter, but now the birds are flown and the nest is empty; the old gentleman who once was a person of consideration and influence but now is pushed aside and forgotten. All these might well think tenderly about the past and look with distaste upon the present. But, on the other hand, how many there are who imagine that life was paradise, let us say before the first world war, and now everything is 'going to the dogs', which is little better than a delusion, a mirage of memory—

> And is it that the haze of grief
>   Makes former gladness loom so great?
>   The lowness of the present state,
> That sets the past in this relief?
> Or that the past will always win
>   A glory from its being far
>   And orb into the perfect star
> We saw not when we moved therein?

Anyhow these, though their talk may be depressing, are not the real pessimists. There are many other varieties. There are the people, readers mostly, who fancy they belong to the lineage of the great pessimists of history, from Diogenes and the Cynics to J. P. Sartre and the Existentialists, passing by Marcus Aurelius the Roman Emperor, Omar Khayyam the Persian poet, other poets like Leopardi, Alfred de Vigny, Byron, Shelley, and the author of the *City of Dreadful Night*, other philosophers like Pascal and Schopenhauer, and the neo-pagan novelists and dramatists of to-day. The follower of these people to-day is the doctrinaire pessimist who looks down with disdain at a mankind deluded with the futile fancy that there is any real good in life and human nature or that society is not doomed to decay and dissolution, if, indeed, it has not already reached that state.

Besides these there is the temperamental pessimist who *voit tout en noir*, who gloats over gloom and is never happy unless he is miserable. Of such men somebody has written: " If you have a wireless outfit you can pick out of the air cries of distress from foundering vessels. Now some men make of themselves highly-sensitized receivers of S.O.S. from every shipwreck of mankind, past, present, or future. They have picked up all the sighs and sobs of history, until life seems a funeral where everybody is a pall bearer just the day before he occupies the hearse himself. . . . Every woe and pain is recorded until mankind seems a festering wound and the earth a huge hospital."(1) They echo all the sighs of the discontented and all the grievances of the disgruntled. They ' take a poor view ' of everything and are sure that the worst *is* coming to the worst.

We might study next the pessimist as prophet—him, too, you may meet with in the byways. He watches the trend of things and invariably forebodes disaster: he outdoes Cassandra. One element only he leaves out of his calculations—the Providence of God.

What makes men pessimists? There are those, as I have suggested already, who are prone to pessimism by temperament and disposition. The old physicists would have said that the melancholy (Greek for black bile) ' humour ' predominates in them. They are built that

---

(1) F. P. Donnelly: *Mustard Seed.*

way. Others are embittered by their experience of life. They expected too much of it, perhaps, and it has played them false. They are disillusioned. With others again it is a pose. Their gloomy view of things gives them an air of profound thinking and marks them off from the common herd of foolish optimists tripping heedlessly along the primrose path to—well, possibly the eternal bonfire. Not long ago a certain writer published a book ([1]) on pessimism in which he sought to prove that the element common to all pessimists is *pride*. Well, that may be true of the doctrinaire pessimist and of the man with whom pessimism is a pose. But I fancy what makes pessimists is, for the most part, too exclusive and too habitual a concentration on the awful mass of misery and evil in the world, to the neglect of all the good it contains. Were it not for this goodness, God knows there is enough wickedness and crime on the one side, suffering and sorrow on the other in the world to make any man a pessimist. G. K. Chesterton, in his Autobiography, admits that he called himself an optimist because he was " so horribly near to being a pessimist ".

We are agreed then, I think, that one who spreads around him an atmosphere of unmitigated gloom is not a helpful fellow-wayfarer for us people of the byways. Shall we then decide to consort with optimists, become optimists ourselves, perhaps? Before deciding, it might be well to pause a little and get our ideas clear as to what optimism is. Well, it might be roughly described as the frame of mind of people who believe, try to believe, or talk as if they believed that everything is all right or going to be all right, as the case may be. Or, in a milder form, and in Wordsworth's words—

> Our cheerful faith that all which we behold
> Is full of blessings . . .

---

[1] *The Nature of Evil.* By Radoslav A. Tsanoff; London, 1932.

As with pessimism, there are varieties of optimism. There is the temperamental optimist who is simply a man of sanguine disposition who likes to look at the bright side of things. There is the deliberate and, as it were, professional optimism of M. Coué and of the Christian Scientists with their ' better and better every day, better and better every way '. These two paragraphs from W. B. Maxwell's *Life: A Study of Self*, hit them off rather neatly:

> " Personally I hate the temperamental optimist. Nothing can be more annoying to one than silly optimistic friends who, bearing the misfortunes of others with a radiant equanimity, tell us that the portmanteau left behind on the platform of a seaside station may perhaps come on by another and faster train and be waiting for us when we get to Victoria.

> " I hate, too, and worse, the optimist who has taken up optimism as a stock-in-trade, who begs one not to cry over spilt milk, who himself ostentatiously smiles and rubs his hands while others weep, who will assure a man stricken to death that things are never quite so bad as they seem and every cloud has a silver lining. This optimistic disregard of stern facts and cheerful embrace of the impossible are more particularly distasteful when they form part of an attitude that has been adopted professionally."

Yes, I think we have all met the professional optimist. He usually takes the form of a commercial traveller (at least in the U.S.A.), the salesman, or the publicity agent, but we come across him in other walks of life as well. The blinkered optimist, as we might call him, haunts the byways no less than the highways. Somebody has described him, not very elegantly perhaps, as the beaming bounder with the sunny smile. This sham cheerfulness in season and out of season is particularly prevalent, it would seem, in the United States, where the "boosting" of optimism has been adopted in certain circles as a deliberate policy.

So the optimism that ignores all unpleasant facts or tries to explain them away is, to say the least, worthless. But is that enough to justify G. K. Chesterton's conclusion in *The Everlasting Man*, " Optimism is morbid; it is even more morbid than pessimism "? Hardly, yet Chesterton's conclusion is not just a paradox. For there are deeper reasons why optimism is false. One of them he elsewhere puts into words—" Christianity began with the assumption that God has come on earth because all is wrong with the world." Well, not quite all, for there was on earth one who was to be His Mother. But let that pass. And we may conclude with another writer: (¹) " There is and can be only one ground [for optimism] and that is belief in a loving God. Apart from that, optimism is a mere will o' the wisp, which depends either on a sanguine temperament or a pathetic trust in human nature, to which the whole of human history gives the lie." But what this writer calls optimism is simply faith and trust in God, free from the deliberate blindness and onesidedness of optimism. It is in fact sane Christian realism, fully aware of all the evil in the world, but undismayed by it, as knowing that God out of evil can draw good and that He must conquer evil in the end. Meanwhile the Christian realist remembers that God looked upon the world He had made and saw that it was good, for He had bestowed upon it something of His own infinite goodness and beauty. May I leave the poet to sum up in his own poetic way (²)—

> Stop and consider! Life is but a day;
> A fragile dewdrop on its perilous way
> From a tree's summit; a poor Indian's sleep
> While his boat hastens to the monstrous steep

(¹) Lindsay Dewar: *What Is the Purpose of Life?*
(²) Keats: *Sleep and Poetry.*

> Of Montmorenci . . . Why so sad a moan?
> Life is the rose's hope while yet unblown;
> The reading of an ever changing tale;
> The light uplifting of a maiden's veil;
> A pigeon tumbling in clear summer air;
> A laughing school-boy without grief or care
> Riding the springy branches of an elm.

Yes, life is not so bad after all!

On the whole, the pessimist is a fellow-wayfarer with whom we might well be rather eager to part company, unless we wish our mental temperature to be lowered, our enthusiasm damped, and our outlook darkened. For pessimism is infectious—if you take the pessimist seriously.

Dr. Downey, Archbishop of Liverpool, said wittily on one occasion: " Pessimists are never happy unless they are thoroughly miserable. They take a worm's eye view of the world." And again, " A pessimist is a man who, when he has to choose between two evils, chooses both."

3. THE CONVERSATIONALIST

I did not care to head this section merely, " The Talker ", but the fact is that, as you go through the byways of life, you will probably hear a vast deal of talk but very little conversation, at least in the best sense of that word. The author of *Lectures of a Certain Professor* wrote, many years ago: " Conversation in any worthy sense of the word is the rarest thing in the world; and people who can judge say that it is becoming rarer every day." That was before the days of the radio and the cinema! Writing much more recently, an Oxford don says much the same thing: " Really good talk is one of the greatest pleasures there is, and yet how rarely one comes across it."[1]

---

[1] A. C. Benson: *From a College Window.*

I fancy that if, in any company you are likely to frequent, you were to give utterance to the above opinion, you might be faced with stares of puzzlement and even of indignation. You would seem either to be reflecting on the conversational powers of those present, or, at best, making a perfectly unmeaning statement. For nowadays, I venture to say, any such distinction between conversation properly so called and any other kind of talk would seem to most a distinction without a difference. Nevertheless, let us, at least for the sake of argument, attempt to maintain the distinction. Let us pass in review some of the types of talkers that most of us come across at one time or another, and leave it an open question whether they are conversationalists or not.

There is first the gossip. By that I do not of course mean the person who engages in ' small talk ' about the weather, the crops, sport, the latest news, and so forth. For at that rate we should all be gossips. It is the person who indulges in more or less idle talk about *persons*—absent ones of course—their peculiarities, their short-comings, perhaps their delinquencies, the usual topic, it is supposed, of afternoon tea, when, as Pope wrote:

A third (speaker) interprets motions, looks, and eyes;
At ev'ry word a reputation dies.

And another eighteenth century writer, Congreve, makes one of his characters say: " Why they (the ladies) are at the end of the gallery, retired to their Tea and Scandal." It is to be feared that afternoon tea and scandal, or at all events gossip, still maintain a certain association even in the middle of the twentieth century. Indeed gossip is considered (by men, of course) a speci-ality, if not a monopoly, of women. Monopoly it certainly is not. Reputations may be laid on the dissecting table in the smoke-room or the lounge quite as readily as on the afternoon tea table. And the talk in these institutions, as we know, does not stop at gossip, but descends to even lower levels. If in some incredible Utopia there were no afternoon teas, no bars nor lounges, and no tobacco, I am inclined to think there would be very little gossip. Moreover, many people would have a great deal more time on their hands. Would they spend it any better? Who can tell?

Then there is the talker whose idea of conversation is a monologue, who holds forth on some subject which happens to interest him, with scant regard for his hearers whom it may not interest at all. He will descant on his grievances, his ailments, his children, or she about the servant problem, the prices of things, her household troubles, to people whom all these things do not affect at all. It is to be hoped that one will listen politely and even sympathetically, though, like Carlyle, one does not find it exhilarating to " sit still and be pumped into ". Unless, as a wit remarked, you may like to hear a man talk about himself because then you will hear nothing but good.(1)

Others there are whose notion of conversation is telling one anecdote after another or seizing upon every remark you make to tell a story more or less *à propos*. This may be interesting enough up to a point, but it is apt to grow wearisome, especially when the teller of anecdotes breaks into a serious conversation with some trifling funny story which may raise a momentary laugh, but interrupts the flow of conversation and may break it off altogether.

You will, of course, have met from time to time the talker who is ready to " take you up " on some casual opinion you have had the hardihood to express, the argumentative one who lies in wait for some saying of yours and pounces on it. Perhaps you are ready to " take him on " and argue the thing out. More often, I

---

(1) Another wit has said: It's all right to hold conversation, but you should let it go now and then.

expect, you are not. You would rather agree to differ.
You are not disposed for a long argument which will
probably end by both holding their original positions,
but in the course of which tempers may get frayed. One
or other may seem to have the best of it, but

> He that is convinced against his will
> Remains of his own opinion still.

Anyhow, argument of the contentious sort is hardly
conversation. After an evening during which the
redoubtable Dr. Johnson had " floored " several conversational adversaries, Boswell records: " When I called
upon Dr. Johnson next morning, I found him highly
satisfied with his colloquial prowess the preceding evening.
' Well ', said he, ' we had good talk '. Boswell: ' Yes,
sir, you tossed and gored several persons '." It is to be
thought that the persons over whom the Doctor
triumphed can hardly have relished that " good talk ".

Dr. Johnson's weapon in this wordy warfare was
somewhat of the bludgeon type. A rapier may be even
more deadly. Wit and sarcasms may cause deeper and
more lasting wounds. Those who possess the gift of
mordant wit are to those who have it not as the brass
pot to the glass vessel. There is a well-known anecdote
of Richard Brinsley Sheridan, himself a noted wit,
telling how, issuing from a certain company where a
luckless victim was being stung and goaded by ridicule,
he turned to one beside him and said: " If that be wit,
then Heaven grant me a double dose of dullness."

You will meet, too, garrulous old people who will
indulge in endless reminiscence about their young days.
And you can hardly hope to escape the bore who will
buttonhole you and hold you till he has told you at
full length one or more of his pointless stories or given
you unasked his views on some favourite topic of his.
Finally there is the man who so enjoys the sound of his
own voice and the outpouring of his notions that he

talks and talks tirelessly, ignoring all attempted interruptions. Of these, A. C. Benson wrote: " People who are fond of talking ought to beware of being lengthy. How one knows the despair of conversing with a man who is determined to make a clear and complete statement of everything. Arguments, questions, views rise in the mind in the course of the harangue and are swept away by the moving stream."[1]

Dean Swift, in one of those ironical, facetious writings of his, *A Compleat Collection of Genteel and Ingenious Conversation* (1738) pretended to prescribe a remedy for tiresome talkers. " When ", he writes, " this happy art of polite conversing shall be thoroughly improved, good company will be no longer pestered with dull, dry, tedious story-tellers, nor wrangling disputers."

What then, one asks, are the qualities of a good conversationalist? They have been described as humour, quickness, the power of seeing unexpected connections, picturesque phrasing, natural charm, sympathy, readiness. Well, perhaps. But qualities such as those are hardly attainable by effort. If one has them, well and good. All depends on the use made of them. More valuable, it seems to me, are just these—a well-stored mind, a pleasant manner, a readiness to *listen*,[2] an interest in the person to whom one is talking, and a power of imaginative sympathy with what he says. Indeed I know of no better advice than that given by the author of those charming essays which he entitled *Lectures of a Certain Professor*.

" The best thing ", he writes, " that you can bring into conversation is *easiness*, to be at one's ease, not excited, not self-conscious nor self-sufficient nor too well-prepared with a view to shining, or displaying

---

[1] *From a College Window.*

[2] Not listless, distracted listening. We hear with our ears, but we listen with our entire body, eyes included. That is what is meant by undivided attention.

knowledge or information. . . . Be just yourself, but
of course your best self. Don't pretend to be what you
are not." In short, conversation is courtesy, and courtesy
is founded on forgetfulness of self.

Thus the quality of one's conversation is of importance
both to others and to oneself. Hardly less important is
the quantity. Here, as usual, there may be error both
by excess and by defect, too much or too little. Too
little conversation means taciturnity and unsociableness.
If you err on that side the loss is mainly yours. Not
so with the much commoner error of excess. What a
vast deal of vapid, aimless, but by no means always
harmless talk goes on the world over, from morning till
night and far into the night. Tongues wag incessantly
just for the sake of wagging. Granted that much of it
provides a sort of safety vent, or shall we say ' exhaust ',
especially for women. But how much of it is sheer waste.

> Words are like leaves and where they most abound
> Much fruit of sense beneath is rarely found

Apart from the botanical allusion Pope no doubt was
right. Not that conversation need always be serious. On
the contrary, joking and light *badinage* is all to the good
when talking is just a needed relaxation. The pity is
that there is so much of it and that it is so often a very
inadequate substitute for better things. With many, one
might almost venture to say with certain nations, it is
a substitute for action. We in Ireland have a gift for
conversation, and revel in it. But what comes of it?
There is a vague feeling that, when all has been said and
well said, something has been *done*. But speeches are
no substitute for deeds, nay, often serve to make deeds
impossible. One resolute man who says little but has
thought things out and knows his own mind can do
more than a swarm of talkers. Talking, too, is often a
substitute and a very poor one for thought and for
study, consuming time that might have been so much

G

more fruitfully spent. Finally, in long drawn-out conversations the tongue, of which small member St. James,
in the third Chapter of his Epistle, has so poor an opinion,
has ample scope for the many delinquencies to which
it is prone. " There are some men ", writes Father
Faber, " who make it a kind of social profession to be
amusing talkers. . . . They are the bugbears of real
conversation. But the thing to notice about them is,
that they can hardly ever be religious men. A man who
lays himself out to amuse is never a safe man to have
for a friend or even an acquaintance. He is not a man
whom anyone really loves or respects. . . . He is for
ever jostling charity by the pungency of his criticisms
and wounding justice by his revelation of secrets. *Il n'est
fas ordinaire*, says La Bruyère, *que celui qui fait rire se
passe aimer* ".[1]

When all is said, the best kind of conversation, the
conversation that really helps us along our way, is the
tête à tête with a friend or congenial companion. Then
alone can we enjoy, unrestrained, that " heart affluence
in discursive talk " which is the greatest charm of conversation. For we have a listener who shares at least
some of our interests and of our dreams. To meet, on
our way through the byways, with such a fellow-wayfarer
is a piece of good fortune for which to be grateful to
God.

4. COMPANIONS AND COMRADES

He Who made men and sent them into this world
provided that they should not walk alone through life,
that they should have companions on the way. That
companionship begins in the warm bosom of the family.
The child, from its first conscious moment, finds itself
the object of the love and care of mother and father,
perhaps too, of sisters and brothers who have come a

---

[1] Father F. W. Faber: *Spiritual Conferences.*

little sooner into the world. The growing boy or girl may soon come to have, outside the family circle, comrades whom they call their 'chums' or 'pals'. But the dear companionship of home lasts on for many a year. Alas, sooner or later, in the nature of things, an end must come to it. With the coming of manhood or womanhood comes the making of a great choice. The normal choice, by God's design, is wedlock. And then there begins a companionship far closer than any other in this world, a companionship that shall be sundered only by death. Those who choose a narrower way, the way of the priesthood, the religious life, or both, enter upon a companionship, or rather, perhaps, a comradeship which is akin to that of an army, based like it upon a common devotedness, but upon a devotedness to a far higher cause.

As life goes on there may come into it another kind of companion and comrade, one whom we call friend. Friendship need not mar the far more intimate companionship of marriage and it may provide companionship to men and women who have never entered upon that state. It may even provide something which not even the family nor wedded love has provided—one of kindred mind who can fully sympathize in distress as well as in joy, who can share confidences that might pain those dearest to us, and who can help to bear certain burdens of the mind, and thereby to lighten them. As Tennyson wrote of his own lost friendship:

> But this it was that made me move
> As light as carrier-birds in air;
> I loved the weight I had to bear,
> Because it needed help of Love:
> Nor could I weary heart or limb,
> When mighty Love would cleave in twain
> The lading of a single pain,
> And part it, giving half to him.

What is here said of human friendship is likewise true of the Divine:

"He bore our sorrows, and carried our griefs."

The friendship I am speaking of at present is not friendship of the sentimental or emotional kind, but what André Maurois, accomplished man of the world as he is, describes as friendship between "two perfectly lucid people who are not physically attracted to one another" but who are kindred spirits, "twins in soul" as William Penn calls them,(¹) with interests and tastes in common, with mutual liking, esteem, and probably admiration, and a steady trust in one another.

If such a friendship is to last and bear its full fruits it calls for certain qualities in you and in your friends. To begin with, it may be that you or the person you would make your friend are unsuited to friendship. "The covetous", says Penn, and we may well agree with him, "the angry, the proud, the jealous, the *talkative*, cannot but make ill friends." For friendship demands on *both* sides forbearance, readiness to give and take, helpfulness, and no small degree of disinterestedness. If so and so is your friend just for what you hope to get from him, used when wanted and neglected when not, you have not made a real friend at all. Once more I call upon William Penn, this time to sum up the qualities of the true friend. "A true friend unbosoms freely, advises justly, assists readily, defends courageously, and continues a friend unchangeably."

That worldly philosopher, Bacon, devotes his essay on friendship to reckoning up its advantages. "It is a mere and miserable solitude to want true friends, without which the world is but a wilderness." He sees in friendship benefits both for the heart and for the mind. For the heart it opens up an opportunity for unburdening

---

(¹) *Some Fruits of Solitude.* This is the William Penn from whom Pennsylvania derived its name.

itself, for we can impart to a friend griefs, joys, fears, hopes, suspicions, counsels, grievances. For the mind it can do two things. In attempting to express and communicate one's thoughts to a friendly listener one clarifies the thought itself. And again, we learn by receiving friendly counsel. " There is no such flatterer ", says Bacon, " as a man's self and there is no such remedy against flattery as the liberty of a friend "—a *candid* friend, one presumes.

Genuine friendship then can mean a great deal to a man. In another chapter of this book (¹) I have dwelt upon its value as an antidote to loneliness. ." Nothing ", says a recent writer, " can save the lonely but warm human companionship." It ought also to be an antidote to selfishness, for, as I likewise say there, friendship is not possible, unless one be prepared to give oneself away to another. To be a friend you must be capable of caring about people, what they think, what they feel, what they suffer. If you are not, you may have acquaintances but not true friends. Again, friendship makes greatly for happiness. " Probably ", says the same writer, " the best definition of earthly bliss is " four feet on a fender ", for friendship is the greatest blessing in life, just as loneliness is the darkest sorrow." No one who has one good friend can be said to have failed in life. There is no more enduring thing in life than real friendship. But it is a plant that has to be cultivated, to be watered and tended. Neglected, it is liable to wilt. " A man, Sir ", said Johnson, on a certain occasion, " should keep his friendship in *constant repair*."

But I find myself writing quite a miniature treatise on friendship without intending it, except in so far as it bears upon my theme of fellow-wayfarers in the byways. Great writers have long ago said most of what could be said about it. It is, indeed, a far cry from Cicero and

(¹) Lonely Spots in the Byways. Ch. IX.

his *De Amicitia* to André Maurois. In between, St. Ailred, abbot of Rievaulx, who flourished in the twelfth century, wrote an entire book about it, a book recently rediscovered and translated into English under the title *Christian Friendship*. It was published in 1942 by the Catholic Book Club of London. Tennyson's *In Memoriam* is one long threnody for a lost friend. If we would bring home to ourselves what friendship meant to one man, we can see it in that poem. Other great elegies— Milton's *Lycidas*, Keats's *Adonais*, Mathew Arnold's *Thyrsis* have likewise been inspired by sorrow for the loss of a friend. These are beautiful memorials of human friendships, but they do not express what is highest in friendship. For this latter you may read in your *Imitation of Christ*, Book II, Chapter 8, "Of Familiar Friendship with Jesus."

The upshot of all that has here been said is this— You will be blest if, on your way through the byways of life, you can meet with one or two good friends and if you can keep them, ever remembering these words of the *Imitation:* "Without a friend thou canst not well live; and if Jesus be not thy friend above all, thou wilt be exceedingly sad and desolate."

(¹) "Life", wrote Dr. Samuel Johnson, "has no pleasure higher or nobler than that of friendship."

CHAPTER VII

RUTS IN THE BYWAYS

" OPINIONS may be prisons and prejudices dungeons. A narrow groove may be as bad as a concentration camp. Certain habits put the soul into a strait waistcoat ". So says a recent writer.([1]) Well, opinions and prejudices are grooves in the mind: habits are grooves in one's conduct. And grooves are like the ruts left by cartwheels in the byways before the days of macadam and even after them. Once the cart or the waggon rolled into such ruts it was not easy for the horses to drag it out again. But can habits, grooves, customs, routine—call them what you will, come to be for us quite as our author, just quoted, represents them? No doubt there are ' bachelor habits ' which are not, I think, in very general favour. Walter Pater committed himself to the aphorism that " to form habits is failure in life ". No doubt those condemned to routine detest it or profess to do so, and it somehow adversely affects their lives. As for custom, Shakespeare makes Coriolanus exclaim:

> Custom calls me to't!
> What Custom wills in all things should we do't
> The dust on antique time would lie unswept,
> And mountainous error be too highly heaped
> For truth to overpeer.

And Montaigne seems to have had an equally poor opinion of custom when he wrote: C'est à la vérité une violente et traîtresse maîtresse d'école, que la coutume." A recent writer notes the present day repugnance for all these things. " There is in our day a desire to escape

---

([1]) Stephen Graham: *Thinking of Living.* (London: Benn, 1949).

93

out of self destroying [i.e., destroying personality, the self] grooves and ruts, to cast off useless traditions, to cut a way through the network of custom and habit in which we are enmeshed."([1])

And yet on the other hand one could quote Pascal, and other writers as well no doubt, on the advantages of custom,([2]) most of the ascetical writers in favour of habits—good ones of course, and something may be said even in favour of routine. So, as there are evidently pros as well as cons to be considered, we must not dismiss the subject too lightly.

To begin, then, with grooves in the mind, that is to say, firmly-held opinions, judgments, convictions. To people, and they are very numerous nowadays—who do not admit any such things as fixed, certain, unchanging truths (except perhaps the latest pronouncements of the scientists), all such grooves are bad and harmful. We must be prepared at any moment to change our "views" about anything whatever (except the latest theories of Science). In fact, according to many such thinkers, truth for me is what I believe to be true and that is all the truth there is—for me. Other people see other "aspects" of truth, and that is the truth for them. No wonder that all grooves of fixed opinions, judgments, and convictions are treated as so many prejudices that fetter our intellectual freedom.

But for Christians who know for certain that there *are* fixed, unchanging truths, in fact a vast field of truth whereon we tread as on firm and solid ground, the existence in our minds of grooves is no matter for

---

([1])Aloysius Roche: *Religion and Life*.

([2]) To cite just one. Philip Hamerton in his well-known *The Intellectual Life* writes: "The business of the world could not be carried forward one day without a most complex code of customs. . . . We ought to think of custom as a most precious legacy of the past, saving us infinite perplexity, yet not as an infallible rule." p. 197. And he goes on to point out the dangers of excessive subservience to custom.

reproach. Nay, the more firmly fixed they are from our early youth the better for our after years. For Catholics, who believe that Christ founded a Church which cannot lead us astray in faith and morals, that firm ground of truth is vaster still.

Still for us Catholics, as for all mankind, there are wide regions in which the light is dim and one's footing less secure. And here it is quite possible that opinions, judgments, and convictions, however strongly held, may indeed be prejudices, mere ruts in our thinking. Yet, even where no light of revelation guides us, we have still the light of reason, still the power to reach certainties, and, when judgments and convictions are based on certainty, why should we decry them? I think our right attitude in life should be a balance between having ' the courage of our convictions ' and being ' open to conviction '. And I fancy that what Pater meant to condemn was wrong-headed intellectual and moral prejudices, based not on reason nor on faith, but the outcome of heredity, environment, mere sentiment, or a fanaticism of some brand or other.

Nevertheless, as it stands, his pronouncement is untenable, and A. C. Benson is surely nearer the mark when he writes: " As a rule it may be said that Pater's dictum is entirely untrue, and that success in life depends more upon forming habits than upon anything else except health ".(¹) If by habits this counter dictum meant virtues—for the virtues are habits, then, no doubt, we could accept it without reserve. But from the remainder of his essay it would seem that that was not quite what the writer meant, though doubtless he would not exclude the virtues. But in any case the obvious fact is that there are good habits as well as bad habits, useful habits as well as useless, and to condemn all habits as such would be merely an absurdity.

(¹) *From a College Window.*

Now I do not intend to discuss the virtues nor the vices: that is for another sort of book. Instead I shall talk of certain habits that are usually passed over in that other sort of book, though not only success in life, as A. C. Benson says, but happiness in our own lives and in the lives of those about us depends upon them quite a good deal. One of these is order or orderliness, some definite order in one's home, one's room, one's office, one's desk. Order in the distribution of one's time. ' A place for everything and everything in its place '. A time for everything and everything at its right time. That is the watchword. It is a habit to be acquired only at the cost of persevering effort, but the effort is worth our while. Another such habit is punctuality, the practice of which calls for a good deal of self-denial, and means much to the comfort and convenience of others. Again, to acquire the habit of foresight is a valuable asset in life from day to day. The old adage comes back to mind—' Look before you leap '. Think beforehand of what you are going to say *and* of what you are *not* going to say. People who rush off on journeys and find when too late that they have forgotten all sorts of things suffer from the want of this foresight. Think ahead! Plan ahead! These are useful maxims. And so one might go on.

But a caution, or rather, several, must be entered here. Habits may tend to become tyrannical over ourselves, and for others " laws of the Medes and Persians which must not be altered ". Those rigid programmes and time-tables with which nobody dare interfere! Even our most praiseworthy habits must on occasion be modified for higher considerations. How much more those little meaningless ways and habits into which people (bachelors particularly) are prone to drift. At best they are oddities, at worst nuisances.

Then there are practices which tend to develop into habits, habits that grow upon one and are difficult to check and more difficult to throw off. Quite legitimate practices in themselves, be it said. Such are the smoking habit, drinking habits, and gambling. One might well pause and think quite a good deal before allowing any of these to become fixed habits. For they mean a veritable slavery, though one be fettered with silken bonds. Because what satisfies a craving, however artificial in its origin that craving may be, has a tendency to increase the craving and gradually to strengthen its grip.

Customs might be described as a sort of collective, communal habits. They are not the creation of one person nor of any number of persons that one could name; nor do they come into existence all at once, but need time to become what they are. The individual does not form them, he adopts them or submits to them. Thinkers dwell upon their great power—Shakespeare, Montaigne, and Bacon, to name three great minds. They can prevail against truth and against morals and against laws. The two last-named writers set forth a series of fantastic and often horrible customs that were and are accepted without demur by whole peoples. For centuries wives in India were burned on the funeral pyres of their husbands (¹) or buried in their graves. It had to be, for that was the custom. For the same reason, in savage lands, men and women submit without question to hideous mutilations and disfigurements. Head hunting and cannibalism were as much part of life as our morning coffee or our after-dinner cigar. Bacon speaks of the reign or tyranny of custom. " Neither nature nor the engagement of words are as forcible as custom. The predominancy of custom is everywhere visible; insomuch as a man would wonder to hear men profess, protest, engage, give great words, and then do just as they have

(¹) This was known as suttee and was eventually prohibited by British law.

done before." They relapse into their accustomed ways. And Montaigne points our how men are made accustomed from infancy to certain usages which come to seem to them all that is right and natural and proper, however unreasonable and absurd they may seem to us.

The same writers, and of course many others, point to another law of custom. That to which we grow accustomed gradually comes to affect us less and less. Montaigne puts it quaintly—" Mon collet de fleurs sert à mon nez: mais après que je m'en suis vêtu trois jours de suite il ne sert qu'aux nez assistants ".([1]) One can grow accustomed to noise—to the roar of passing trains, to the thunder of bombardments, till a time comes when one can hardly sleep without them.

Again, *assueta vilescunt*,([2]) familiarity breeds if not contempt, at least indifference, the cessation of wonder and awe. Custom stales. " Science ", says a recent writer,([3]), " does not dispel mystery, or if it eliminates one mystery, it does so only by substituting for it a still greater mystery. . . . If it were not for the deadening influence of custom, we should be like Alice in Wonderland, in a perpetual state of surprise." Tennyson makes the speaker in his *Locksley Hall* 60 *Years After* complain that

Half the marvels of my morning triumphs over time and space
Staled by frequence, shrunk by usage into commonest
commonplace.

" Innumerable ", wrote Carlyle, " are the illusions and legerdemain tricks of Custom: but of all these, perhaps the cleverest is her knack of persuading us that the Miraculous, by simple repetition, ceases to be miracu-

---

([1]) My garland of flowers serves my nose, but, after I have put it on three days running, it only serves the noses of those around me.

([2]) What we are quite used to comes to be held cheap.

([3]) Kenneth Walker: *Venture with Ideas* (London: Cape, 1951).

lous. . . . Am I to view the Stupendous with stupid indifference because I have seen it twice or two hundred or two million times? " St. Augustine notes how men cease to wonder at God's daily marvels, such as that of human birth, the coming into existence of a human soul out of nothingness, a thing, he says, more wonderful than the raising of human beings from the dead, but less regarded merely because more frequent.([1])

" To us ", says another writer,([2]) " the world grows stale because in proportion as we become accustomed to a thing we are estranged from it. In proportion as we win the daily presence of our friends we lose them. We come to regard life as a dry packet of facts. We want the spirituous refreshment of another's vision. We want to have our eyes reopened and our souls made naked to the touch of being."

If it is so in the contemplation of nature, it is so also in the ordinary affairs of daily life. And it is quite liable to be so in the practices of religion. Gradually they may cease to move us till they become little better than mechanical.([3]) Unless we vigorously react or receive some strong stimulus from without, religion may become to us mere conformity and a matter of routine.

But, as Pascal points out, there is another side to this matter of custom. In the *Pensées* he recurs to the subject in several passages, but there is one in particular in which he sets forth his idea very clearly. I venture to quote it in full:—

([1]) Majora miracula sunt tot quotidie homines nasci qui non erant quam paucos resurrexisse qui erant: et tamen ista miracula non consideratione comprehensa sunt sed assiduitate viluerunt.

([2]) Max Eastman: *The Enjoyment of Poetry.*

([3]) As Dr. Hedley remarks incidentally in his *Retreat*, " Any face, any scene, however striking, loses its stimulating power over the human faculties when they have become accustomed to it."

" We must not deceive ourselves: we are automatons ([1]) as much as minds; whence it comes that the instrument or means by which conviction is brought about is not solely logical proof. How few are the things that are proven! Proofs convince only the mind. Custom provides us with our strongest and most widely-believed proofs; it bends in a certain direction the automaton that is in us and that draws with it the mind without its being aware. Who has demonstrated that it will be day to-morrow or that we shall die? And what is more believed than such things? It is therefore custom that convinces us; it is custom that makes so many people Christians, it is custom that makes Turks, pagans, trades, soldiers, etc. (as contrasted with Turks, Christians have the faith received in Baptism). In fact, once the mind has seen where the truth lies, one must have recourse to custom so as to soak ourselves with this belief which is ever tending to escape us; for to have the proofs always present is too much to expect. We must acquire an easier belief which is that of habit which without violence, without artificial stimulus, without argument makes us believe things and bends all our powers towards this belief so that our soul naturally falls in with it. When we believe only by dint of conviction and the automaton that is in us tends to believe the contrary, that is not good enough. We must therefore make both parts of us believe: the mind by reasons which it is enough to have realized once in our lives; the automaton by custom which we must not permit to tend in a contrary direction. *Inclina cor meum Deus.*"([2])

([1]) That is, I take it, moved as it were blindly by something within us, instinct, custom, hereditary prejudice, and so forth.

([2]) Ps. 118, v. 36, in the Douay version reads " Incline my heart into thy testimonies."

It may be that Pascal uses the word custom here in a more pregnant sense than is usual with us. It was, I think, St. Augustine who first said that habit was second nature, a modification of our nature that ends by becoming an element in our personality. Elsewhere in the *Pensées* Pascal writes: "*La coutume est notre nature*", and taken in that sense we can accept the thought of the passage I have quoted. His conviction by custom and conviction by logical proof reminds one somewhat of Newman's distinction between real and notional assent. But if you would pursue the matter further I would refer you to that great thinker's *Grammar of Assent*.

Certain it is that our faith (not only our religious beliefs but our convictions generally) is greatly sustained and strengthened by awareness of the faith of those among whom we live and is, on the contrary endangered in a milieu of unbelief. To the latter fact many a Breton peasant in Paris and many an Irish worker in England are only too faithful witnesses.

Lastly we come to routine which we might call the rut *par excellence* if that did not sound rather like a contradiction in terms or else the figure oxymoron! Many hard things are said about routine, and some of them, no doubt, are justified. It has been accused of narrowing and even stultifying the minds of those subjected to it. It has been described as the chief source of that monotony which is one of the banes of life. Hence the craze for change at all cost, adventure, the new and strange whether in real life or in the cinema. People say they are sick of doing the same old thing day after day and over and over again. Hence more and more extended week-ends, more and more prolonged holidays.

I have no wish to deprecate all that. But I would point to one or two other aspects of routine and monotony. In the first place it is, in the conditions of modern life and industry, inevitable. Huge numbers of human beings are, in one way or another, geared to the machine, not only operatives but whole establishments which employ machinery. And even apart from machinery, how can there be order and efficiency and departmentalisation in the office or the bureau or the Civil Service without routine? And can it be denied that this routine has a value of its own for the individual? Is it not a sort of education in discipline (sadly lacking in other walks of life) and in team-work? There are people, no doubt, who hate discipline because they love their own sweet will and who hate team-work because they are individualists. But are these to be considered as models or even as normal people? However, I am not so ' optimistic ' as to think that discipline and team-work are likely to be loved for their own sakes. But there is a higher way of looking at them. There is, for instance, the concept of duty and a sense of loyalty to the undertaking in which one is engaged, be it a firm or a government. There is the sense of pride in one's task, however monotonous, and the resolve to do it perfectly, to make it a success as far as in us lies. These are fine ideals as far as they go.

But one might go further. As it has been well said, it is not so much external happenings that give our lives the tinge and tang of excitement, emotion, romance. It is our inward attitudes of imagination, heart, and will. And the thrill of adventure is to be judged, not by what one is doing or what is happening to him, but by what is going on within him. Take the example of love. A man is engaged in some monotonous and boring occupation, tied down by routine. He marries, and all is transformed. His work is now a source from which he wrests a livelihood for the woman he loves and for their children.

It is henceforth imbued with emotion and romance. His life from day to day has taken on a new meaning.

> Love took up the harp of life and smote on all its chords with
> might,
> Smote the chord of self that, trembling, passed in music out
> of sight.

And so it can be with those for whom patriotism, religion, the love of God, enters into the monotonous routine of daily life.

ENVOI

A Prayer Against Use and Wont.

I who these sixty years have seen
    The pageant of the months unrolled,
The woods put on incredible green,
    The common decked in fabulous gold—

I never hurl my hat on high,
    I turn no cart-wheels for sheer mirth;
What should so crass a thing as I
    Do crawling between heaven and earth?

A myriad tapestries of cloud
    Drape hour by hour day's awful arch,
A myriad blazing spear-points crowd
    Night's plain with march and counter-march.

Seraphs whose dreams outreach the stars
    Sit with me in my morning train;
They rest or writhe in fleshly bars,
    They tread unscathed through hells of pain.

For me, since twice ten thousand dawns
    Have borne such wonder on their wings,
What gulf of black dishonour yawns,
    Who feel no rapture at these things?

Gross, formal, vacant, pampered, sleek,
    Why was I dowered with birth and **breath**?
Lord, let me *live* a year, a week,
    An **hour, a** moment, ere my death!

Nevile Watts.

H

A Further Note on Habits

Habits are studied in philosophical treatises both under the heading of psychology and under that of ethics. Habit is generally defined as a disposition that is stable, at least relatively so, gives facility, and is acquired by repetition of acts. A man has ten fingers, clumsy, awkward, all thumbs, as the saying goes. Then comes habit and works its way into flesh and muscles and joints and nerves, till at last those clumsy fingers can fly like lightning over a keyboard. How much laborious practice and repetition goes to that result only the learner can know. This is an *active* habit, due to something done by the person who acquires it. On the other hand there are *passive* habits due to some cause from outside the person. These again are of two kinds— those which are purely passive such as sounds to which one gradually grows so completely *habituated* that one hears them no longer or is not aware that one hears them. This is the kind of habit that tends to destroy wonder, surprise, delight, romance, and also to lessen pain. And again there are passive habits with which a man co-operates such as drug-taking, drinking, smoking, and many other things.

Habit has a great variety of effects. One can become so used to hardship or suffering as in the end hardly to feel it. One can become so accustomed to pleasures that one becomes *blasé*, or, as we say nowadays, " fed up ": they have lost their zest by dint of too frequent repetition. A habit may grow stronger by what it feeds on, as in the case of the tippler or the drunkard or, in a milder way, the smoker. Habitual acts end by becoming a *need*. Dr. Samuel Johnson allowed himself to fall into the queer habit of touching every post he passed. In the end he could not pass a post without touching it, and, if by any chance he missed one, he felt so uncomfortable that he had to turn back in his walk and repair the omission. Habit is a good servant but a bad master.

Habits, then, can be evil and dangerous. But, on the other hand, they can be a really valuable asset in life. They are nature's method of getting things done with increasing ease: all depends on whether these things are worth doing. And this ease is seldom attained without conscious effort. Obvious examples are punctuality, regularity, order, politeness, even cleanliness. The average small boy, I think, positively delights in being grubby and tousled: he resents having to wash his hands and to brush his hair. The natural man hates having to rise at a fixed hour, especially if it be early, dislikes being " tied down ", finds it irksome to put each thing back in its place instead of dropping it where he last made use of it, likes to " take his time " and do things just when " the spirit moves him ". But this doing of things we dislike, is it not part of that self-discipline which our wayward nature needs? More than that, is it not part of our Christian denying of self and taking up our cross? Are these things too trifling to be worthy of our efforts? " He that is faithful in that which is least is faithful also in that which is greater ". So spoke the Master.

After all, one of the essentials of a soldier's training is drill—the dull repetition of seemingly useless actions. Does the " soldier of Christ " need no such training?

It is interesting to note that all our faculties may in one way or other become subject to the laws of habit. We have already remarked that our feelings, our sensitive being, may by repetition of acts grow accustomed to suffering or else to happiness. Our passions, by frequent yieldings to them, may become ungovernable, or by frequent acts of repression and control, may be mastered. The mind or intellect plays a considerable role in the perception of our senses. For instance, sight gives us merely coloured extent, but, by repeated associations, it comes about that through sight we gain information about the temperature of a given object, on its three dimensional shape, its distance from us, and so forth. Of its own nature the hearing gives us mere sounds, but again by repeated acts of association and comparison we come to know the nature, distance, position, etc., of the object or person emitting the sound. Again, thought grows accustomed to processes of abstraction, reflection, analysis, reasoning, etc. Putting, as we say, two and two together, it reaches certain conclusions which may be of great value to us. The study and practice of logic helps the mind to exercise itself in these processes.

The will, on its side, can likewise be exercised and trained by repeated acts. As the proper object of the intellect is *truth*, so that of the will is *good*. It naturally tends to what is presented to it as good. Good presented in this way can become a motive of action, and it should be our aim to accustom ourselves to, to form the habit of, acting from the highest motives.

The fact that repetition of acts is necessary for the acquisition of habits has given rise to such sayings as *faber fit fabricando*, or *en forgeant on devient forgeron*, practice makes perfect, such and such is an " acquired taste ", and so on.

* * * *

In *The Education of Character*, by Father M. S. Gillet, O.P. (later Master General of his order) there are several valuable chapters on habit, pp. 121-164.

What Habits Have You? by Father Robert Nash, S.J., is a practical and helpful booklet which I would recommend to all readers. It is published by the Irish Messenger Office, 6 Great Denmark Street, Dublin.

* * * *

" The unfortunate thing about this world ", wrote Mr. Somerset Maugham, " is that good habits are so much easier to get out of than bad ones."

CHAPTER VIII

OF MUSTS AND THE SECOND MILE

As we go on our way through the byways—and even along the highways, of life, there is one thing we are sure to experience sooner or later, and that is compulsion. We *must* go this way or that, we *must* keep to this side of the road and not the other, we *mustn't* go through this gate or cross that field, we *must* hasten here and go slow there, we *mustn't* halt at this point nor enter that house. We should much prefer, of course, to wander at our own sweet will and trudge unhindered along our *petit bonhomme de chemin*. But it is not to be, and so, like tourists in Germany or France confronted by vexatious notices beginning with *Verboten* or *Défense de . . .* , we are apt to fret and fume, to grumble and ' grouse ' and otherwise express our feelings in language not always printable. But we generally have to obey.

Many years ago somebody lent me a little book entitled *The Second Mile*. I actually returned it to its owner! But I retain some of the wise things I read in it. The book took its name from a sentence spoken by Christ and recorded in the Gospel. " Whosoever ", He said, " shall compel thee to go one mile go with him two."([1]) Rather an exacting demand, to say the least of it, you may think. But let us see.

We may as well face the fact that not only travelling the roads, but, as we say, at every hand's turn compulsion must be accepted as a permanent feature of human life. We have all got to knuckle under and submit to it. The body says *must* and may not be gainsaid. The demands

([1]) St. Matthew, v. 41.

of life with others say *must*. The exigencies of business, of one's occupation in life, say *must*. The limits of one's abilities and opportunities say must *not*, in no uncertain terms. Nor need we be surprised if the moral law, too, says its must and must not.

Fashion, too, says must; so does convention, various social taboos (as we say, borrowing a term from negro religion) are just so many must nots. It is in vain that a man strives to shake himself free from the compulsions that press in upon him from all sides.

Youth makes many a valiant effort to free itself—to scorn convention, to defy taboos, to burst the barriers that seem to hem it in. Nothing, it thinks, can stay its onward march. No summit seems beyond its reach, no goal too distant to attain, no destiny, however splendid, beyond achievement. Alas, long before youth has passed, the young man may well have learned a lesson, one that need not embitter life, nor dash his hopes, nor scatter all his dreams, but one that is salutary and in any case inevitable, the lesson that on every path on which he may venture there are barriers, some no doubt obstacles that may be vanquished, but many that are impenetrable. His way is shut in, perhaps by hedgerows only, perhaps by stone walls too high to climb.

Now in what attitude of mind shall I acknowledge my barriers and meet my musts? To rave at them, to fret and chafe, is as foolish as it is useless. What if we were to take the advice that Wisdom gives us—go the second mile, be twice as willing to act as compulsion is to force us? Only by an unstinted willingness to do more than anyone lawfully demands of us do we measure up to a true Christian standard. And when we meet compulsion like that, lo! all the sting of compulsion is gone.

Let us, in the light of that saying of Christ, look at some of those compulsions that none of us can elude.

There is first the compulsion of *time*. We are apt to fret at time's inexorable passage, mourn our lost youth, chafe at the inevitable limitations of age. Why not greet age with the cheerfulness of Rabbi ben Ezra—

> Grow old along with me,
> The best is yet to be,
> The last of life for which the first was made.

True, age can be vain and garrulous and self-centred, and there is no fool like an old fool. But I think it is the normal thing that the old have gained from the passage of time and experience qualities that youth can hardly win; they are kindlier, more tolerant, more serene, their minds are richer and deeper, mature and seasoned like old violins and old wine. So when age comes let us accept it not with resignation only but with gratitude.

Then there is the compulsion of *work*. Shall I accept it doggedly and be " beaten to it by the cat-o'-nine-tails in the hands of necessity "? Shall I work just the bare needful with my eyes on the clock? Well, that is one way. But, if I believe that work is the lot of all men, and so the will of God, my Father's business, and in itself an ennobling thing, not a slave's drudgery, then I shall be twice as willing to work as compulsion is to make me. I shall go the second mile with it. I shall say, like the great violin-maker, Stradivari, in George Eliot's poem:

> If my hand slacked
> I should rob God, since He is fullest good,
> Leaving a blank instead of violins.

There is manifold compulsion, too, in the circumstances that may confine our lives to narrow and obscure activities, in short, to the byways of life, and in the limited abilities which forbid us to hope for greatness. In early years we may fancy ourselves ' mute inglorious Miltons ', genius unrecognized, Napoleons that lack but opportunity to rise to glory. In our day dreams we saw ourselves playing a great part in the drama of life. If we be any of the things we fancy, our day may come. Meantime it were better for us to face the cold realities, better to accept our circumstances, at least ' on account ', to accept our personality with all its unescapable limitations. But again, let it not be mere resignation—' what can't be cured must be endured ', nor even just making a virtue of necessity. We can do better than that in the spirit of the Second Mile. Let us welcome and rejoice in our circumstances, not other circumstances but *these*, however narrow and unhelpful. ' I shall profit by these circumstances in which I find myself '. Moreover, I shall make the most of this one talent which God has given me to start life withal. I shall not whine for more talents nor repine at the lack of more. I shall wield this one talent as Samson wielded that famous jawbone of an ass. Others may look around them and feel " cabined, cribbed, confined ", without scope to deploy their abilities. I shall work in intensity if I cannot expand in space. You remember that sonnet of Wordsworth's:

> Nuns fret not at their convent's narrow room,
>   And hermits are contented with their cells,
>   And students with their pensive citadels;
> Maids at the wheel, the weaver at his loom.
> Sit blithe and happy . . .

Aye, and prisoners have found in their gaols contentment and even stimulus to their genius. To gaols we owe *Don Quixote* and the *Pilgrim's Progress*, Mitchel's *Jail Journal*, *I Miei Prigioni*, and *De Profundis*.

We enter next the sphere of duty and moral obligation. The most of men think mainly and even solely of their rights. These they are ready to maintain against all comers. Are they not God-given, indefeasible? But duty seems an unlovely being even when reluctantly acknowledged as the " stern daughter of the voice of God ".

What duty *demands*, that we shall do, but not a whit more. (You remember, perhaps, that character in Gilbert and Sullivan's opera who was ' the slave of duty '). But the spirit of the Second Mile can make of duty a joy instead of a slavery. Indeed, it is only when the voluntary saturates and overflows the compulsory that life ceases to be a bondage and reaches its true meaning. Not till duty looms larger than rights is a man in the full sense Christian. Translate duty into privilege and at once it ceases to be a burden. That is why The Master's yoke can be sweet and His burden light.

But one thing only can make every yoke sweet and every burden light, and that is LOVE.

May not a man then stand up for his rights? He may, by all means. No law human or divine forbids him. Only let him be sure that they *are* his rights, that no *higher* rights take precedence of them, and that he perform the duties that are the counterpart thereof.

And as with our duties, so it is with the whole sphere of moral obligation, beginning with the Ten Commandments. One may spurn and defy them all, for man is free. One may yield to them as under sheer compulsion— "needs must when the devil drives!", resenting the most of them as mere fetters on our liberty and a muzzle on our personality, but deciding that it is safer to obey. Or one might meet them in the spirit of the Second Mile. God knows the Law of Moses and its elaborations in later days put many a shackle on men's liberty and laid many a burden on their backs. Yet we find among the Psalms a hymn to the Law whose 176 verses are one long cry of praise of that Law and of joy in it:

> O how have I loved thy law, O Lord. It is my meditation all the day long.
> I have had understanding above ancients because I have sought thy commandments.

How sweet are thy words to my palate, more than honey to
    my mouth.
Thy word is a lamp to my feet and a light to my paths.
I meditated on thy commandments which I loved.
I opened my mouth and panted: because I yearned after thy
    commandments.
I have hated and abhorred iniquity; but I have loved thy
    law.
Much peace have they that love thy law.

Yet that was under the Old Law, the law of fear rather
than of love, before the gentle voice of Christ had uttered
the Sermon on the Mount and all the other words that
go to make His teaching, before He had said at the
Last Supper, " this is my commandment that ye should
love one another as I have loved you." The spirit of
Christianity is to go beyond what God commands, to
forgive seventy times, to pray for enemies and bless them
that curse us, to act as no man has a right to demand
of us, and feel, like Christ Himself, that our meat and
drink is to do the will of Him who sent us into this
world.

One could almost classify people according to the
spirit of the Second Mile. There are the people who
say " I must ", the slaves of compulsion; the people
who say " I ought ", the grim moralists doing their duty
with conscientious woodenness; and the people who
cry " I want to, let me at it ", with their sense of privilege
in life, for whom all duty is a glorious prerogative. They
" delight in the law of the Lord ". It is because of their
unwillingness to go the second mile that the first two
classes make such desperate bones about going the first.
They are " just as good as trying not to be bad can
make them ". And it is because the third is willing to
go the second mile that his well-doing is a joy and not
a burden. It is hard work serving as a conscript in a
war you would fain have shirked, but it is a glorious
business fighting as a volunteer for a Cause you love.

CHAPTER IX

LONELY SPOTS IN THE BYWAYS

LONELINESS is a distressing experience which well-nigh all of us pass through at one time or other in our lives. It may come upon us in childhood. It surely comes to orphans and to the only child who is jealously kept apart from playmates, and to children unwanted or misunderstood. One thinks of Florence Dombey, the Mighty Atom, and other such children in fiction. But in real life such loneliness is only too common and quite as poignant, I think, as loneliness ever is in later years.

It may come to young people whose occupation throws them among strangers far from their homes, to the emigrant, and to the exile in a foreign land, and of course to that most unhappy product of the late war, the " Displaced Person ". Unmarried men and women, unless surrounded by friends or caught up in some absorbing task or in some great cause, must have their hours of loneliness. All must suffer bereavements which, for a time, make the world seem empty and life a blank—the loss of father and mother, wife or husband, or some idolized child. But time heals the sorest griefs. Then as life goes on and friends become estranged or die, first the dear old friends of our early years and the kind indulgent uncles and aunts, then the school companions of our boyhood, then the friends and acquaintances we have made in manhood, we feel more and more the void around us, and grow lonelier. We that are left are mere survivors. Is it not time for us too to go?

> Why linger, why turn back, why faint, my heart?
> They have departed: thou shouldst now depart.
> Follow where all have fled.

Yes, but in God's good time. Meantime, as I hope to point out in the last chapter of this book, there may lie before one many fruitful years, years, even to advanced old age, filled with public service, literary activity, or works of zeal and charity.

There are, of course, the self-satisfied, pushful, " hard-boiled " people who never feel lonely. They have no time for that sort of thing. And there are those who all their lives long are lonely or rather solitary, natures that are shy, reserved, sensitive, introspective, or merely self-absorbed, who make few friends and who shun crowds and assemblies. Indeed, there is nowhere that one can feel so lonely as in crowds, above all in the crowded streets and resorts of great cities where one has no friends. For " a crowd is not company and faces but a gallery of pictures, and talk but a tinkling cymbal, where there is no love." Whereas in what most people would call solitude we may not feel loneliness at all. In these two stanzas of Byron the contrast is expressed; rhetorically, if you like, but truly enough:

> To sit on rocks, to muse o'er flood and fell;
>   To slowly trace the forest's shady scene,
> Where things that own not man's dominion dwell
>   And human foot hath ne'er or rarely been;
>   To climb the trackless mountain all unseen
> With the wild flock that never needs a fold;
>   Alone o'er floods and foaming falls to lean
> This is not solitude, 'tis but to hold
> Converse with nature's charms and view her stores unrolled
>
> But 'mid the crowd, the hum, the shock of men
>   To hear, to see, to feel, and to possess
> And roam along, the world's tired denizen,
>   With none to bless us none whom we can bless;
>   Minions of splendour shrinking from distress!
> None that with kindred consciousness endued,
>   If we were not would seem to smile the less
> Of all that followed, flattered, sought, and sued;
> This is to be alone, this, this is solitude.

It were well with us, indeed, if by taking refuge with nature we could find solitude but cast off our loneliness. Personally I can well believe that we may sometimes do so. The sudden realization of the selfishness, the forgetfulness, the lack of understanding, the unfairness, the ingratitude of those around him might weigh a man down with loneliness. And in such moments he might well find solace in nature like the child of whom Wordsworth wrote—

> And hers shall be the breathing balm
> And hers the silence and the calm
> Of mute insensate things.

And in a similar vein a very different writer, Mr. Hilaire Belloc—

> " In deep woods and there alone you may wholly cut yourself off from the disturbance of human society and the catch and pull and drag of daily things."

But can one always thus rid oneself of loneliness? There are those who imagine that travel and change of scene can always drive it away. And if their troubles come from without, they may indeed thus find relief. But often loneliness arises from within, rising like a mist in the damp hollows, and then it is vain to hope for so simple an escape. Socrates, on being told that an acquaintance of his had returned from travel and seemed no better for it, drily remarked; " I do not wonder: he took himself along with him." If a man, because of some inward state of soul, is not at peace with God nor with his fellow men, little wonder that he should feel a loneliness that can be cast off by no change of place or occupation.

Even, however, if for the moment we pass over the conscience that is lonely because of the lost friendship of the only Friend whose friendship must never be forfeited, there is a loneliness of a man's own making, the loneliness of one who has no friends because he does not know how to make friends or how when made to keep them. Leaving aside again those rare beings who have a vocation to solitude,([1]) may we not say that loneliness comes of the lack of friends, that making friends is a habit, the habit of giving oneself away to others.

It seems to me, then, that there are two things that hinder the making of friends. One is that a man is unwilling to give himself away.([2]) That unwillingness surely implies a forgetfulness of the truth that friendship to be real friendship must be mutual. "Love", writes St. Ignatius Loyola, in his *Exercises*, "consists in mutual interchange on either side, that is to say, in the lover giving and communicating with the beloved what he has or can give . . . and thus the one shares everything with the other." He does not confine this to divine love, nor need we. It is true of the love of husband and wife and it is true of friendship. And greatest of all the things one "has or can give" is himself, his trust, his confidences, his self-revealment in whatever manner he may care to make it. Gifts and mutual services are of but little account compared with that mutual giving of oneself.

The other hindrance to the making of friends is to form so lofty, so exacting a notion of the ideal friend that none of those around us can measure up to it—or so we think, and accordingly we search the horizon for an ideal friend. Years can pass like that and still the unending search goes on, till we have reached the low, dark verge of life and find at last that it is now too late for friendship. Why not begin to form the habit of friendship by making friends with those nearest to us? Granted that none of

---

([1]) That the most of men have no such vocation is clear from the effects upon the human spirit of solitary confinement. Some who have suffered it have written accounts of its horrors.

([2]) L'amitié, writes Pere Sertillanges, O.P., consiste à transporter son moi en autrui.

them quite measures up to that high ideal of ours. Granted that among them there may be minds so alien, so uncongenial to ours that they could never be real friends. These latter are surely the exceptions. No less surely enough remain on whom to exercise whatever gift of friendship may be ours. Call them, if you will, not friends but acquaintances. What matters the name so there be something of the substance of friendship underneath it. If you do not even seek their acquaintance, how shall you come to know whether they be worthy of your friendship?

Nor must we wait for others to seek us out. Let us go to them, loving as God loves according to St. John: " Beloved, herein is love, not that we love God but that he first loved us."(¹) Let us try to imitate Christ's friendship which went forth no doubt to the holy women, and to John the Beloved, and to the rest of the Apostles, but also to publican and sinner, to the outcast and the shunned of all men, to the woman who was a sinner in the city. He did not anxiously enquire whether such people were worthy of His friendship. " Ye are my friends ", He said, " if ye do the things that I enjoin on you." That little token of good will was all He asked: it is all He asks of us. Ought we to exact from those whom we would make our friends more than we are prepared to give them?

There are those who, in default of friends, look elsewhere for companionship in their solitude. Some find it in nature, not so much perhaps, the wild nature of field and woodland, but rather some garden of their own. Some seek it from animal pets, to say the least a harmless hobby. Yet one finds oneself at times regretting the care and affection lavished upon dogs and cats, affection that might have been poured out on human beings. Happily there are those who solace their loneliness with these

---

(¹) I John, iv. 10.

dumb companions and yet can spare affection and helpfulness for human neighbours too and for the poor. Others again there are who find in books the best companions of their solitude. Whether or not they have been frustrated in their search for friendship, they can, through books, make acquaintance with kindred minds and form a pleasant sort of friendship with the heroes and heroines, real or fictional, of whom they read.

But whatever be the companionship that we choose in order to make up for the lack of friends, it is well to teach ourselves betimes first to endure, and then to enjoy, a measure of solitude. For solitude in itself is good for us. Many of the Saints from St. Paul onwards loved the desert or longed for it. Not only those whose vocation was solitude like the solitaries of the Thebaid in the early centuries, the Céili Dé in Ireland, and the Carthusians even to-day, but also men of action who from time to time fled from outward activities and the haunts of men into silence and solitude. They felt that solitude brought them somehow nearer to God and gave them insight into their own souls. Perhaps the greatest value of what is now familiar to us as a retreat is just this solitude. No doubt those who make retreats listen to the considerations put before them by a director or, in default of that, read spiritual considerations from some book. But it has been said, and there is truth in the saying, that so many days passed in silence and retirement without help of director or even of books would be of more value to a soul than the same number of days with such help but without the silence and solitude.

For the generality of people, however, such a spiritual retreat is a rare experience, yearly at most, and lasts but a little time. It is not enough to teach one the love of solitude. Fortunate is the man, one of the few, who can contrive a little sanctuary for himself—his office, his study, his den, where he can be alone, solitary and yet not lonely. In the Abbé Dimnet's book *The Art of Thinking* there is a chapter (p. 91 and following) in which he dwells on solitude as an aid not only to thinking but to living. " The Art of Thinking ", he writes, " is the art of being one's self, and this art can only be learned if one is by one's self."

But when all is said we must expect to feel loneliness from time to time. We may have our dark days. Such moods and moments come when it is borne in upon us that we are exiles here below and that the place of our final sojourning may be yet a great way off. And such moments are good for us if they foster in us that detachment, that " sitting light " to passing things, which ought to be natural in a Christian who believes in a never-ending hereafter. Such moments came even to the Master himself, in the Garden when He uttered the sad reproach, " Could you not watch an hour with me? ", and on Calvary when He uttered that cry of anguish, " My God, My God, why hast Thou forsaken me? "

When we think of a loneliness such as that, how slight, how trifling seem our moods of loneliness. For instance, the form of loneliness that I may call, perhaps, the Cinderella feeling, the impression, real or imaginary, that one is being left out of things, passed over, forgotten. All of us, no doubt, have felt this at times. We do not always feel that there is a reason for it. Could that reason be our own shortcomings, for instance our lack of social gifts, of entertainment value? In that, at least, there is no moral fault and with that consideration we can console ourselves. There may be other reasons, of course, but what of it, after all; there is One who will never pass us over, never neglect us nor forget us. We are always in the kind hands of God.

Indeed when believing Christians suffer more than merely passing moods of loneliness, it may be because they forget for the time that they can say with Christ

J

Himself: " I am not alone because the Father is with me;" because they fail at the moment to realize that One who said: " I have not called you servants but friends," "sitteth at the right hand of the Father in Heaven" and never for a moment forgets even one of us.

Take up your *Imitation of Christ* and read Book II, chapter 8, and having taken it up read also Book I, chapter 20, of the Love of Solitude and Silence.

CHAPTER X

HARDSHIP IN THE BYWAYS

SOME THOUGHTS ON CROSSES

THOUGH this word " cross " may seem to you to savour too much of the language of spiritual books, I nevertheless chose it as a title and that for two reasons—first because it covers all the ills that both flesh and spirit are heirs to—suffering, sorrow, bereavement, physical pain, illness, disappointment, failure, and the rest of them, and then because it symbolizes the significance of all that.

People of the byways are wont at times to look with envy at the great, the prominent, the prosperous, fancying that pain and sorrow can hardly touch them, that they have the power to fend off all suffering from their lives. It is a delusion and a somewhat childish one. Have these people, for instance, no bereavements? Can they ward off death? or disease? Have they no disappointments? nor disillusions? No jealousies, no quarrels, no estrangements? Does the possession of a great name or a great fortune or a reputation for great learning carry with it no cares and anxieties? Has it not been said ' Uneasy lies the head that wears a crown '. Aye, even if that head be not destined to the fate of a Mary Queen of Scots, or a Charles I, or a Louis XVI. This writer, too, like all his readers, has had his sorrows, bereavements, disappointments, and so forth. Suffering, it is true, has not played so to speak a leading role in his life and so, perhaps, he may be permitted to stand aside and to allow others who have "known sorrow and become acquainted with infirmity " to speak out of the heart of their experience, while I add a comment here and there.

First, then, in partial justification of my title, there is this:—

"The first rays which pierced the dark abyss of suffering streamed forth from the Cross, from that conception of the world and of life that is distinctively Christian."[1] Suffering, he goes on to point out, was thus revealed as (1) A divinely appointed means of victory over sin. (2) A proof of God's love and mercy. (3) Fruitful in its hidden power to make expiation for the sins of others. (4) A goad to quicken our steps in the way of salvation (Hebr. XII, 10). (5) A means of grace (1 Peter, I, 20). (6) A witness to divine love (Hebr. XII, 5). (7) A process of moral purification and restoration (Rom. V, 3. 2 Cor. XII, 7).

These, of course, are only headings and would need development and even proof, for some of them sound paradoxical. No doubt the passages which I shall presently quote will go far to justify these statements or at least point towards a justification.

Two basic truths must ever be kept in mind:—

This life here below is not our only life, it is not even our true life, but only a time of trial and probation for the life to come. Yet, as such, it is to us of enormous importance.

Secondly the only real, unqualified, evil in this world is sin.

Looked at from the point of view of these two truths suffering and sorrow are in the first place instruments of our trial. As St. Peter writes in his first epistle when reminding the Christians of the glorious reward that is in store for them: "At the thought of which you exult, though . . . you have suffered for the moment from various trials, so that the genuineness of your faith, a thing more precious than gold which though perishable has to be tested by fire, may win praise and glory and

---

[1] Tillman Pesch, S.J.: *The Christian Philosophy of Life*, Ch. cxliv.

honour." This is a theme that recurs not infrequently in the New Testament.

Accepted in the right spirit suffering teaches one the seriousness of life. Without it, men might take all things lightly, like children looking on the world as a playground. Sorrow sobers us, stirs, at least for a time, the depths of our being. " Prosperity ", says Bacon, " doth best discover vice; but adversity doth best discover virtue." Even extreme misfortunes—deformity and blindness, prison and long illness, may throw one in upon oneself and give time to think of the deeper things of life.

Sin is the only real evil in the world. Suffering is both the result of sin, a possible expiation of sin, and a means to lessen sin. It is the result of sin because it was the primal Fall that brought into the world death and concupiscence, roots and origins of all the miseries to which man is heir—disease, bereavement, temptation, guilt, and sin with all its hideous train of suffering and anguish. Suffering is the punishment brought upon the human race by sin, but this suffering may be turned to glorious gain, if accepted with humble submission and offered in expiation and in union with the sufferings of Christ. " Now I rejoice ", wrote St. Paul, " in my sufferings on your behalf, and make up in my flesh what is lacking to the sufferings of Christ (viz. our participation in them), on behalf of his body which is the Church."([1]) When the Apostles were arrested by the Sanhedrin and scourged, " they went forth from before the Council rejoicing that they had been counted worthy to suffer dishonour for the Name."([2]) And the history of martyrdom all down the centuries shows that the martyrs accepted not merely with submission but with rejoicing and exultation torture and death. To them suffering was at once an expiation for their sins, a proof of their love of

---

([1]) Epistle to the Colossians, Ch. I. 24.

([2]) Acts. V. 41.

Him for whom they suffered and died, and an identification of themselves with the Passion of the Great Martyr.

And quite apart from martyrdom we note in the lives and writings of the Saints an attraction to suffering and an extraordinary gift of rejoicing in it. Speaking on behalf of Christians in general (though it is true they were then all prospective martyrs) St. Paul wrote to the Romans; " We exult in our tribulations, knowing that tribulation worketh endurance, and endurance strength of character, and strength of character, hope, and hope doth not prove false." (v. 3.). St. Teresa with her prayer *aut pati aut mori*, " O Lord, either to die or to suffer ! I ask of Thee nothing else for myself," might almost be taken as typical of the attitude of God's heroes towards suffering. They have felt it shame to be " delicate members of a head crowned with thorns." And they added to the ordinary sufferings of life self-inflicted austerities that make us shudder. After all, did not Christ Himself say " Blessed are they that mourn ". From that saying of His stems all that the spiritual writers have said in praise of suffering. Such is that lofty panegyric in the *Imitation of Christ*—The King's Highway of the Holy Cross. (¹) And many modern spiritual books develop the same theme. If you are a sufferer and even if you are not, you would gain by reading one or other of them. Here are a few titles:—

> *The Art of Suffering*, translated from the French of Louis Bertrand. (London : Sheed and Ward).
>
> *I Give Glory*. A Book for the Sick, a translation of that very consoling book by the Abbé Henri Perreyve, *La Journée des Malades*. (London : Sands).
>
> *The Mission of Pain*, translated from the French of Père Laurent (London : Burns & Oates 1910). This is an older book and you may have difficulty in obtaining it unless you are fortunate enough to find it in some library.

(¹) Book II, Ch. 12.

Suffering. By Père Laurent de Smet S.J. adapted from the French original by Sister Mary Reginald Capes O.S.D. (London : Sands).

A Key to Happiness : The Art of Suffering. By Marguerite Duportal. (Milwaukee : Bruce).

The Problem of Pain. By C. S. Lewis. (London : Bles).

Comfort for the Sick. By Clara Tiry. (Foundress of The Apostolate of Suffering). (St Louis : Herder).

Man's Suffering and God's Love. By Mgr. J. Messner, translated from the German. (London : Burns Oates & Washbourne).

The School of Suffering. A Companion Book to *More Joy* by Rt. Rev. Wilhelm von Keppler. (St. Louis : Herder) 1929. (¹)

Now we people of the byways who are not Saints nor likely to be martyrs may perhaps be pardoned if we look at suffering from our lower level. It is but human, after all, to shrink from pain and but natural to do all we can to stave off or to mitigate suffering. God will not hold that against us. He knows that often the most we can obtain from ourselves is patient endurance of sorrows and sufferings when they come. Only let our endurance be, not a Stoic hardening of ourselves, but Christian patience, a patience not wholly unmindful of Him who suffered far beyond the utmost limits of our endurance, and that *for us.* Not unmindful, too, that sufferings come from a Father who loves us and, so to speak, has at heart our welfare. In reality, if (but only if) we accept them as such, sufferings and crosses are gifts and graces.

But though this is true, it must be admitted that we do not always find it easy to bring ourselves to see things in that light. So it may be not unhelpful to set down some thoughts of writers who are not looking at things from so supernatural a standpoint. The poet Browning sees in

---

(¹) A further list of books will be found in Appendix B.

suffering and hardship something that hardens and braces the character for the struggle of life

> Then welcome each rebuff
> That turns earth's smoothness rough
> Each sting that bids nor sit nor stand but go.
> Be our joy three parts pain!
> Strive and hold cheap the strain;
> Learn, nor account the pang; dare, never grudge the throe.

As suffering bravely borne goes to the making of character, so it is a test of the same. Here is an incidental sentence from a literary essay: I leave you to work out its implications:—" Suffering cheerfully borne is the ultimate test of artist, lover, and saint alike."(1) Suffering, because it is apt to turn a man from heedlessness to sober reflection and wean him from the lighter side of life to its serious aspects, has often been the means to conversion. It was so to François Coppée who entitled the narrative of his conversion *La Bonne Souffrance*.

Certain of the ancient pagan philosophers, Plato included, realized by the unaided light of reason that every sin calls for punishment, and so they taught their disciples not to shirk suffering, nay to welcome it, as a punishment and consequently an expiation of their sins. The Stoic philosophers taught their disciples to face danger, sickness, suffering, and death itself with an impassive and defiant courage. Such an attitude may seem fine from the purely natural point of view and it has many modern admirers. Nevertheless it is not the Christian attitude.

One precious consolation in suffering, sorrow, and bereavement is the thought that time is a wonderful healer. The agony cannot last: it will pass away, and, for the most part, leave no lasting or bitter memory behind. And here I shall quote two passages which may make a fitting ending to these few thoughts:—

---

(1) In *Poets and Pilgrims* by Katherine Brégy.

" And then, too, if we have suffered, as we all must suffer, if we have any heart or blood or brain at all, we can learn the blessed fact of the utter powerlessness of suffering to hurt or darken us ... Once over, it becomes instantly either like a cloud melting in the blue of heaven, or, better still, a joyful memory of a pain that braced and purified. No one ever gives a thought, except a grateful one, to past suffering. If it leaves its handwriting on brow or cheek, it leaves no shadow on the spirit within." So wrote A. C. Benson in the Epilogue to his book *The Silent Isle*. And Sir Edwin Arnold writes in *The Light of the World:*—

When all is known,
And the Eternal Wisdom whispers,—glad,—
Its secret to the soul laughing to learn
Death was so friendly, and the toils of life
So fruitful for all living things; and pain
Seed of long pleasure; and, our worst of woes
So like the foolish anguish of the babe
Whereat the mother, loving most, smiles most.

*   *   *   *

To those to whom some great suffering or sorrow has come I venture to recommend the prayerful, thoughtful reading of the narrative of Christ's Passion in the Gospels. And then in the days that follow they could hardly do anything more comforting than to read or dip into that well-known little book—*The Consoling Thoughts of St. Francis de Sales* or else the chapter entitled " Crosses " in *St. Francis de Sales in His Letters* (London: Sands, 1933).

CHAPTER XI

HOMELY WISDOM FROM THE BYWAYS

ONE of the less-known works of the Rt. Rev. Dr.
Richard Chenevix Trench of Dublin, author of the well-
known works on the Parables and on the Miracles of the
Gospel, is *On the Lessons in Proverbs*.[1] From it I cull
the following passage which will serve as an introduction
to what I have to say.

" What a body of popular good sense and good
feeling is contained in the better, which is also the
more numerous, portion of them (i.e., proverbs):
What a sense of natural equity, what a spirit of
kindness breathes out from many of them; what
prudent rules for the management of life, what
shrewd wisdom . . . what frugality, what patience,
what perseverance, what manly independence, are
continually inculcated by them. What a fine knowledge of the human heart do many of them display;
what useful, and not always obvious, hints do they
offer on many most important points, as on the
choice of companions, the bringing up of children,
the bearing of prosperity and adversity, the restraint
of all immoderate expectations. And they take a yet
higher range than this; they have their ethics, their
theology, their views of man in his highest relations
of all, as man with his fellowmen and man with his
Maker." Elsewhere while again calling attention to
their wit, their wisdom, their poetry, the delicacy,
the fairness, the manliness which characterize so
many of them, he admits that there are other

---

[1] London: Parker, 3rd edition, 1854.

proverbs coarse, "selfish, unjust, cowardly, profane."

It must have been this kind of proverb that was most familiar in R. L. Stevenson's experience. Else he could hardly have written the following passage in *Virginibus Puerisque*.

"Most of our pocket wisdom is conceived for the use of mediocre people, to discourage them from ambitious attempts, and generally console them in their mediocrity. And since mediocre people constitute the bulk of humanity, this is, no doubt, very properly so. But it does not follow that the one sort of proposition is any less true than the other or that Icarus (¹) is not to be praised and perhaps more envied than Mr. Samuel Budgett, the Successful Merchant . . ."

Yes, true enough, mediocre people, if by that he means people who are not of outstanding ability and endowments, do constitute the people of the byways and therefore the bulk of humanity. But the moral worth of these mediocre people may be higher than that of the geniuses. Be that as it may, proverbs necessarily embody a philosophy for the average man, since they are a product of the folk mind and would never have achieved universal currency had they expressed the philosophy of supermen. Moreover, as we shall see, proverbs do *not* always encourage mediocrity.

Many of the proverbs familiar to us to-day have come down to us from remotest ages. Generation after generation has recognized their truth and wisdom and has passed them on to the next. Hundreds of years before Christ, the philosopher Aristotle spoke of them as the legacy of ancient wisdom. Our Lord Himself quoted

---

(¹) The Icarus of classic myth who attempted to fly like a bird and fell to his death.

current proverbs, recognizing their truth.([1]) They constitute an " abstract and brief chronicle " of human experience coming down to us from time immemorial. They are current among all peoples, not always in the same form, but often shaped by the genius, wit, and spirit of a particular nation. Literature abounds with them. Some great writers—Chaucer, Erasmus, Montaigne, Shakespeare, Cervantes, delighted in them. They have been quoted and still are quoted as clinching an argument or determining a course of action, almost with the same finality as if one were quoting a text of Scripture.

These wise saws and shrewd adages come, as I have said, from the people, the plain folk, the people of the byways.([2]) They are not a product of the great ones of the highways, the Philosophers, Economists, Sociologists, Critics, Financiers, Big Businessmen. And I fancy these people have little use for them. But we of the byways still cling to them, still warn or console ourselves and one another by repeating them. For we feel that they are not mere dull commonplaces, but, as A. C. Benson called them, " crystals shaped from a thousand human hopes and fears."

Time and again collections of proverbs have been made, proverbs of this or that people, proverbs of this or that author, proverbs of all nations. One collector claims to have brought together some 26,000 proverbs, and neither he nor any other collector has claimed that his collection is exhaustive or complete. Any reader of this chapter as well as the writer of it could call to mind, if he made the effort, scores of proverbs that he has heard quoted. Let me devote a few pages to refreshing the reader's memory and my own. Having refreshed our

---

([1]) " Physician, heal thyself "; " One soweth, another reapeth."

([2]) " Proverbs form a branch of that great mass of folklore that is more especially the possession of the humbler denizens of our towns and rural districts." F. Edward Hulme: *Proverb Lore.*

memory of the words of those once familiar proverbs, perhaps we shall proceed to take them to heart and act upon them.

Let us begin with a handful of cautionary proverbs, proverbs of warning and prudence. They were probably quoted to most of us by our elders when we were young. But they hold good for older people too. ' Look before you leap ' may be good advice for small boys jumping over ditches, but it is also good for young men or women contemplating marriage and for Presidents or Prime Ministers contemplating war. ' Prevention is better than cure ' is a very wise saying not always taken to heart even by officers and Ministers of Public Health or by the police authorities. The " cure " costs the State very dear and often turns out to be no cure at all. The Americans have twisted the adage into ' An ounce of prevention is worth six pounds of coroner's inquest '. ' Let sleeping dogs lie ' applies in many other situations besides that of sleeping dogs. Don't go out of your way needlessly to arouse hostility and opposition—that is the abstract form of it, but how much more vigorous and memorable is the proverb itself. Another cautionary proverb is ' better be sure than sorry ', which fits a multitude of situations, from making quite sure of the date and hour of a given meeting or appointment to taking no chances when otherwise a great opportunity might be missed. ' Make hay while the sun shines ' is almost an application of the last proverb. Here is now the farmer's opportunity. If he does not make sure of it he may be very sorry for himself later on. Seize the favourable moment is the proverb in abstract terms, but in that form it is merely a truism.([1]) How often were our impatience and hurry as young people rebuked by our elders with ' the more haste the less speed '. We lived to realize how true it is in every

---

([1]) The proverb ' Strike the iron while it is hot ' is the blacksmith's version of the same proverb.

department of life. *Festina lente*, hasten slowly, was the old Latin proverb. Some times we get it in the form 'easy does the trick' or in the more dubious form ' Fair and easy goes far in the day ', which might be taken as an invitation to mere laziness, though not so meant.

We probably heard in childhood, if not later in life, the adage ' Waste not want not '. The writer remembers as a very small child being put standing on a table and reciting

> Ladies and gentlemen it is a sin
> To peel a potato and throw away the skin—

on the rather doubtful ground that

> The skin feeds the pigs
> And the pigs feed you . . . and so forth.

I have never quite understood whether the evil consequences of wastefulness were of the economic, or the moral, order.

To take a few further examples of prudential proverbs, ' Once bitten twice shy ' or, in the other form, ' the burnt child dreads the fire ' is even better expressed in the French ' chat échaudé craint l'eau *froide* '. Even the very look of water whether hot or cold would be enough to frighten the scalded cat. That is not so much a cautionary proverb as one that a man quotes to excuse his caution— experience has taught him to be cautious. As a warning against aiming too high or grasping at too many things— you can take it either way, there is the French proverb 'Qui trop embrasse mal étreint'. When there were signs of our eating more than was good for us, we were told that ' enough is as good as a feast '. It might be quoted for anybody who is discontented with moderate means. And when we were pernickety about our food and refused to eat of this dish or that, the example of the other children was pointed out and we were told ' What's sauce for the goose is sauce for the gander '. To which we might have retorted that we did not happen to be either a goose or a gander, or, more devastatingly, ' What's one man's meat is another man's poison '— whatever about ganders. Another piece of common-sense prudence is expressed in the adage ' a stitch in time saves nine '. Even great states have failed to take that proverb to heart. If they had, we should not have heard so often the complaint ' too little and too late '. Another proverb for statesmen no less than for common men is ' Do not count your chickens before they are hatched ' or as a Scottish proverb puts it ' At the end of the game the winner is seen '.

It would, of course, be a mistake to suppose that all proverbs or even the majority of them are of the safety first order. There are also proverbs of encouragement to patience and endurance. ' What can't be cured must be endured ' is good sense but by no means lofty Christian advice. ' Rome wasn't built in a day ' is true enough but not always appreciated by impatient people. The French form is milder 'Petit à petit comme l'oiseau fait son nid, ' a proverb that might come home with greater force to somebody who had happened to watch birds in the process of nest building. ' Well begun is half done' or ' The beginning is half the battle ' may be said to those daunted by the prospect of some big undertaking. And to those who recoil before some seemingly or pretendedly impossible task, ' Where there's a will there's a way '. And indeed to a man of real determination impossible is a word hardly recognized in his vocabulary and obstacles are there simply to be overcome. Of a different order but likewise encouraging to patience is ' No cross, no crown '. A motto for the suffering or the sick is, ' Be the day never so long, at last it cometh to evensong '. An Italian proverb says explicitly ' The world is his who has patience '. And for those who suffer from neglect, real or imagined, and who feel themselves passed over there is the Persian proverb, ' A stone that is fit for the wall is not left in the way '. Prepare yourself, fit yourself to fit in somewhere and you will have a good chance not to be ' left in the way '.

Popular wisdom, though certainly prone to caution and fond of counselling patience, sometimes rises higher and strikes a bolder attitude. We see it in such a saying as ' Nothing venture nothing win ', though that indeed is the outcome of experience like the rest. Again ' Faint heart never won fair lady ' nor anything else. Somewhat akin are the sayings 'No pains, no gains' and 'No sweat no sweet'. There are a great many people who are not alive to the truth that money is best earned by work and usually not earned at all except by work. As the Turkish proverb puts it, ' It is not with saying Honey, Honey that sweetness will come into the mouth '. Another proverb against the over cautious is ' He that hesitates is lost ' sometimes literally, like people who hesitate when crossing a line of traffic, sometimes figuratively like people who by hesitation let slip some golden opportunity, or fail to strike at the decisive moment. Reasonable self-reliance is approved in ' God helps those that help themselves '. *Aide—toi, le ciel t'aidera*, say the French. Was it not Cromwell who exhorted his army before Dunbar, ' Trust God, but keep your powder dry '? It is good theology enough, but much finer is the Irish ' God's help is nearer than the door '.

Some proverbs adopt a caustic tone. They express a rather low estimate of average human nature. Such is the proverb which Trench considers to be the queen of all proverbs, ' The road to Hell is paved with good intentions '. Again ' Promises are like pie-crusts, made to be broken '. Or (a French one this) ' One has always enough strength to bear the misfortunes of one's friends '. A cruel Scottish-Gaelic proverb says that ' Every foot will trample on a man who is in the mud '. I fear there is

a good deal of truth in it, however cruel it sounds. Here
are two Irish-Gaelic proverbs that have something of
this caustic tone—' The best hurlers are on the ditch '
or its variant ' A good boatman is the man on dry land ',
and ' If you want to proclaim (or shall we say broadcast ?)
something, tell it as a secret to a woman '. Almost cynical
is ' Live horse and you'll get grass ' which is not a peculi-
arly Irish proverb since we find Sancho Panza, Don
Quixote's proverb-quoting squire, saying, ' Die not, O
mine ass, Spring will come and with it will come the
clover '.

This last is a good example of how nations often give
a national twist to a proverb that is really international.
There are other examples in plenty. Thus, ' It is an ill
wind that blows nobody good ' appears in Irish as
' There comes no wind out of the sky that does not fill
somebody's sails '. ' Never look a gift horse in the
mouth ' appears in French as ' One must not look at the
bridle of a gift horse '. But this is really a perversion of
the proverb, a proverb which can be traced right back to
St. Jerome. The point is that the receiver of the horse
ought not to inspect its *teeth*. *Noli equi dentes inspicere
donati*. The Dutch version of the hurlers on the ditch is
' The best pilots are ashore '. Their version of promises
and pie-crusts is ' He keeps his word as the sun keeps
butter '. Instead of ' making mountains out of mole-
hills ' the Gaelic proverb says ' Making a great ocean of
a narrow strait '. ' Half a loaf is better than no bread '
is more neatly put in Irish, ' Is fearr leath nà meath ',
i.e., a half is better than want, or lack.

Drink, or rather drunkenness, is, as we might expect,
the target for many proverbs. Thus among the Dutch
proverbs we find ' Full bottles and glasses breed swearers
and asses '. ' When drink is in the man his wisdom's in
the can '. ' The baker cannot be where the brewer is '.
' Who weds a sot to get his cot will lose the cot and keep

the sot.' The Scots say ' A red nose makes a ragged back '. ' When drink's in, wit's out '. Another proverb says somewhat too severely ' Drunkards have a fool's tongue and a knave's heart '. Here is one more, ' The first draught is for thirst, the second for nourishment, the third for pleasure, and the fourth for madness '.

And now just one more sheaf of proverbs. There is the familiar ' Charity begins at home ', a much misused saying which is taken to mean I (or we) must look after myself (or ourselves). Of course, as Trench observes, " what were that charity worth which did *not* begin at home, which did *not* preserve the divine order and proportion and degree? " The nearest and dearest come first but not first, last, and all the time. It must not stop at the limits of the home circle: it must go out to the neighbour, to all with whom we come in contact, for ' our neighbour is all mankind '. Then ' honesty is the best policy ', an outrageous saying if it meant that policy is the only or even the chief motive for honesty. But surely it does not. It means that honesty which is of course morally right, turns out in the long run to be *also* the most prudent course of action. A fine proverb and one of the most pregnant is ' *Noblesse oblige* '. Nobility whether it be that of rank or that of family worth, urges or ought to urge a man to noble, high-minded conduct in keeping with his antecedents. More, all Christians are children of God: to them, too, *noblesse oblige* applies. Another true, and even at first sight obvious, proverb is ' Two wrongs don't make a right '. When some person is accused of wrong-doing and answers his accuser with a ' *tu quoque* ' or, ' but so-and-so (or even everybody) does it ', it is open to the accuser to retort with ' two wrongs don't make a right '. No, but that truth will not prevent people from continiung to act or at all events to talk as if they did.

Indeed I fear that the old proverbs generally are more or less in the same case. Whether it is that they are worn out by constant use and have lost their edge, or that newer sayings largely American have taken their place, too often we hear them but we heed them not. Yet they have not lost their truth nor their wisdom. There are those, too, who make little of proverbs as being purely this-worldly, concerned with time alone and not with eternity. That is true enough of the great majority of them. Yet perhaps readers of this chapter may agree with me that the proverbs set forth therein make for right and goodness, for prudence and patience, for honour and loyalty, and thus are at least contributory to the higher life. Were men to take them to heart and live according to them, I think they would make the world safe for Christianity as we once thought to make it safe for democracy.

*　　　*　　　*　　　*

I leave readers to work out for themselves the implications of a few more proverbs:—' The devil finds work for idle hands to do (a problem of unemployment!). New brooms sweep clean. Least said soonest mended (silence as a first requisite of reconciliation!). Who tries to please everybody pleases nobody, (governments take notice!). Too many cooks spoil the broth, None so deaf as those who won't hear. He that gets the name of early rising may lie in bed late (Gaelic), Qui s'excuse s'accuse, Cut your coat according to your cloth, Don't judge a book by its cover. There's many a slip 'twixt the cup and the lip Nobody but the wearer knows where the shoe pinches. Many a mickle makes a muckle, say the canny Scots, and we with Shakespeare may repeat ' All's well that ends well '.

It would hardly be helpful, I think, to set down here a long list of books about proverbs, as could easily be done. Instead I shall name a select few.

> *Proverb Lore* by Edward Hulme (London : Elliot Stock, 1902) is a worth while book which ought to be easy to find in libraries.

> *The Oxford Dictionary of English Proverbs* is a standard reference book and likely to be kept in print.

> *A Miscellany of Irish Proverbs* by Prof. T. O'Rahilly (Dublin: Educational Co. of Ireland) 1922.

> *Stevenson's Book of Proverbs, Maxims, and Familiar Phrases.* (London : Routledge, 1949.) A really important book.

> *Racial Proverbs.* By Gurney Champion (London : Routledge, 1938.) Some 26,000 of the best proverbs taken from nearly two hundred languages.

> *Scots Proverbs and Rhymes* by Forbes MacGregor (Edinburgh: Moray Press, 1949.)

> *Hand-picked Proverbs.* Selected by Cecil Hunt, illustrated by Blampied. (London : Methuen, 1940.)

> A book entitled *Wit and Wisdom of Don Quixote*, before me as I write, has an index of the proverbs in the book. It was published by Sampson Low in 1882.

*   *   *   *

Maxims, apopthegms, aphorisms, epigrams, and such like sophisticated sayings are for the people of the highways much what proverbs are for our fellow wayfarers in the byways. Collections of such wise or witty sayings abound. Such are those of La Bruyère, La Rochefoucauld, and Montesquieu in French, those of Balthasar Gracian in Spanish. Many of Dr. Samuel Johnson's aphorisms will be found in Boswell's famous *Life*.

CHAPTER XII

" THE SERE AND YELLOW LEAF "?

SHAKESPEARE, or rather, perhaps, his creation Jacques, has drawn a melancholy picture of old age.

> The sixth age shifts
> Into the lean and slippered pantaloon,
> With spectacles on nose and pouch on side,
> His youthful hose, well saved, a world too wide
> For his shrunk shank; and his big manly voice,
> Turning again towards childish treble, pipes
> And whistles in its sound. Last scene of all,
> That ends this strange eventful history,
> Is second childishness and mere oblivion,
> Sans teeth, sans eyes, sans taste, sans everything.

Well, which of us could not point to many an old man who bears very little resemblance to that picture? But let that pass. Shakespeare in any case is concerned only with the ageing body. The mind within is hardly mentioned save perhaps in the reference to second childhood. A more modern poet has more cheerful things to say:—

> Ah, nothing is too late
> Till the tired heart shall cease to palpitate.
> Cato learned Greek at eighty, Sophocles
> Wrote his grand Oedipus, and Simonides
> Bore off the prize of verse from his compeers,
> When each had numbered more than four score years.

> * * * *

> Goethe at Weimar, toiling to the last,
> Completed Faust when eighty years were past.
> These are indeed exceptions; but they show
> How far the gulf-stream of our youth may flow
> Into the arctic region of our lives,
> Where little else than life itself survives.

139

Yes, these are no doubt exceptions, but that they are not quite so exceptional as Longfellow may have thought has been shown by an industrious American librarian, who has compiled a list of ' Men and Women who have Performed Distinctive Service after the Age of 74 ". Let me pick out of her quite extensive list a few names likely to be familiar to most of my readers or specially interesting from some other point of view. And we may be able to add a few more examples as we go along.

To begin with statesmen, we can easily name four or five who have presided over the destinies of their respective nations at a very advanced age. There was Georges Clémenceau, the " Tiger ", who was Premier of France from his seventy-sixth to his seventy-ninth year, during the fateful years of the first world war, and who then presided over the Peace Conference. He died at 88, but his last years were not inactive, for he published his *Demosthenes* at 85, *American Reconstruction* at 87, and *In the Evening of My Thought* in the year of his death.

Our second example is Von Hindenburg, who was President of the Weimar Republic of Germany from his 78th to his 86th year. President Masaryk of Czechoslovakia died at 84. And we had with us but lately the grand old man who was President of Ireland at the age of 85. Going a little back into history, we could find many examples—Gladstone, the Grand Old Man *par excellence*, was Prime Minister for the fourth time from his 83rd to his 85th year and delivered a memorable speech on the Armenian massacres two years before he died at 89. There was the famous Benjamin Franklin, too, of American Revolutionary fame, who was President of Pennsylvania from 79 to 82 and was extremely active to the last. In our own times the feats of agility of Charles Waterton after the age of 80 are almost past belief.[1] A few years ago Gustav, King of Sweden,

---

[1] See *The Squire of Walton Hall*, by Philip Gosse (London: Cassell, 1940).

played tennis with the Irish Davis Cup team at the age of 88. Bernarr MacFadden (patriarch of physical culture) did a parachute jump from 4,000 feet at the age of 81.

Some people might expect *authors* to live long as not living a very strenuous or a very dangerous life. Well, perhaps so, but if they do live long one might expect that their literary gifts would be exhausted long before the end. But certainly it has not always been so. Not a few have not only reached old age and died almost with the pen in their hand, but have made noteworthy contributions to literature in their last years. One of the most surprising examples is the late George Bernard Shaw, who produced in his 85th year a book full of the old verve, clarity, and sardonic outlook so strangely combined with utopianism. George Bancroft, the American historian, produced at 82 his *History of the Formation of the Constitution of the United States.* Walter Savage Landor " read the Odyssey in the original after 85, and wrote in pure and powerful English some of his most wonderfully conceived Imaginary Conversations after he had reached his 89th year ". Oliver Wendell Holmes published between 75 and 80 *Over the Teacups* (which sounds rather juvenile), and several other works. Thomas Hobbes, the philosopher, was engaged in a series of controversial writings on mathematics and physics from about 78 to 90. To somebody who asked in a review of Lord Bryce's *Modern Democracies*, " Has any other man ever produced a work of some twelve hundred large pages, the result of laborious study and travel at the age of 82 ", our foregoing sentence might seem a sufficient answer. But somebody else, who wrote to the *Times Literary Supplement*, suggested that the example of von Ranke, the German historian, was even more remarkable. In 1879, at the age of 83, when weakness of the eyes made him almost entirely dependent on readers and secretaries, he *began* a Universal History of which he completed seventeen volumes before his death seven years later at 91. I can quote an example nearer home. Father Edmund Hogan, S.J. after a long life of writing and research, began the great work of his life, his *Onomasticon Gadelicum*, at the age of 70.

But what of poets? Surely the springs of poetry run dry in old age, and indeed long before it? Well, it is not always so. A modern poet, Robert Bridges, published his greatest, or at all events most ambitious poem, *The Testament of Beauty*, at the age of 85, and he had published five other books after his seventy-fourth year. Tennyson wrote " Locksley Hall " in his youth and lived to write " Locksley Hall Sixty Years After ". I noticed some time ago a review in the *Literary Supplement* of a book of poems entitled ironically enough *When the World was Young*. The author certainly was not, for he was 90. Yet the reviewer was able to write that no reader of those verses would guess from the quality of their style that their author was so old. For there was no sign in them of failing faculties or a hand that was losing its cunning. Thomas Hardy, after a long career as a writer of fiction, gave it up in his last years and took to poetry. He published *Late Lyrics* (they certainly were!) at 82, and three more volumes before he died at 88.

Even the artistic inspiration does not always fail a man in his advanced old age. Giovanni Bellini painted one of his greatest pictures at 75, Corot some of his best after his 74th year. Titian painted several portraits after 80, his " Transfiguration " and " Annunciation " at 90 and the " Battle of Lepanto " between 94 and 98! After that, G. F. Watts painting many pictures after 74 and completing a statue of Tennyson at 85 is almost an anticlimax. Musicians, too, could be quoted who composed even at a very ripe old age. At about 85 Verdi composed his " Ave Maria ", " Stabat Mater ", " Te Deum ", and much else beside. Elgar conducted an orchestra from his death-bed at 76. Saint Saens played and conducted in public after his eightieth year, dying at 86. Sarah Bernhardt, the great actress, played in "Regine Armand" at 76 and in " Daniel " at 78. She died the next year. Macklin (né McLaughlin), the Shakespearian actor who died in 1797 at the age of 107, acted the part of Shylock for the last time when he was 99! On the vigil of Pentecost, 1949, Mrs. Helen Preston Keating of White Plains, N.Y., aged 91, sat down at the piano in a studio in Manhattan and played five double-faced recordings including several compositions of her own. After the hour spent making records, she played for another hour a series of pieces by Mozart, Chopin, and Beethoven. Mr. Eden Phillpots, author of 250 novels, published *Through a Glass Darkly* at the age of 90, and his reminiscences later still.

It is noteworthy that a man who has a great life interest, be it music or science or literature, keeps it up even to extreme old age. J. H. Fabre, the naturalist, carried on his studies and observations until past 90. Sir Isaac Newton, we are told, was working as hard at mathematics and astronomy in his 83rd year as in middle life. W. H. Hudson, writer about nature, published six or seven books after 74, while the great German traveller and explorer, Alexander von Humboldt, wrote his *Kosmos*, an encyclopaedic account of the physical universe, between his seventy-fifth and his ninetieth year. Sir Oliver Lodge published a long series of scientific works after 74, and was writing articles for reviews in the year of his death at 86.

We have all known of great men of the Church who were active even at a great age. Pope Leo XIII was still mentally vigorous at 93. Cardinal Gibbons published at 82 *A Retrospect of Fifty Years*, and at 83 became President of the National Catholic War Council. Cardinal Manning's "intellectual vigour and vision

survived unto the end (at 85) unbroken and unclouded ".
And Cardinal Newman's almost to the end at 89. At 98
Mgr. Langan of Moate was mentally and physically
vigorous and attended to all his duties. He went by air
to Rome in 1950. Many similar examples among the
clergy will be known to readers. Perhaps the clerical life
is one in which a man could be more useful to others at
an advanced age than he could in any other calling.
Even preaching, which, however, does demand a certain
vigour and freshness, may be continued almost to the
end of a long life. Wesley, we are told, was still preaching
almost every day at 88. And in this connection the
following newspaper paragraph may be of interest:
" The oldest Church of Ireland clergyman—the Ven.
John Healy—will be the preacher to-morrow at Morning
Service in St. Patrick's Cathedral, Dublin. Dr. Healy
has just celebrated his 92nd birthday anniversary . . .
When our representative saw Archdeacon Healy in a
Dublin hotel yesterday he said with a smile, ' My health
is as good as ever, but my sight and hearing are not
quite what they used to be.' "

Nearly all the examples I have mentioned are of men
or women of some public note. Much more numerous,
I feel sure, are the cases of persons in private life who
have not only preserved their faculties but have done
useful work at an advanced age. I remember having
pointed out to me some years ago a solicitor who went
about his business very actively at the age of 90, and
about the same time I used to see hurrying along on foot
with his bag of instruments a well-known Dublin doctor
who, I was assured was not far off the same age. Every
now and then there appear in the newspapers photo-
graphs of centenarians. We are commonly told that
their memory is quite clear and their other faculties well
preserved, but we are not often told what activities they
had been engaged in or what work of value they had done.

But here are three who in one respect at least may be said
to have done their duty to the world—Mrs. Vincent J.
Comeau, a native of Nova Scotia, recently observed her
107th birthday. Despite her age, she is in full possession
of her faculties. She has four of her ten children living as
well as ninety-five grandchildren and two great-grand-
children. Mrs. H. —— has been married twice and had
thirteen children, of whom the eldest is 78, and seventy-
two grandchildren. At 101 she reads the daily paper
without glasses. Mrs. L. —— of Malahide, Co, Dublin,
who had twelve grandchildren and twenty-five great
grandchildren celebrated not long ago her 104th birthday,
having just recovered fully from an operation.

His friends and he himself delight in telling us, about
such and such an old man, that he is still hale and hearty.
The fact that he is still alive is just as remarkable. As
Stevenson writes, " By the time a man gets well into the
seventies, his continued existence is a mere miracle ".
And he goes on to ask: " Do the old men mind that, as
a matter of fact? " He answers for them, " Why no."
They were never merrier; they have their grog at night,
and tell the raciest stories; they hear of the death of
people about their own age, or even younger, not as if it
was a grisly warning, but with a simple childlike pleasure
at having outlived someone else; and when a draught
might puff them out like a guttering candle, or a bit of a
stumble shatter them like so much glass, their old hearts
keep sound and unaffrighted, and they go on, bubbling
with laughter, through years of man's age compared to
which the valley at Balaklava was as safe and peaceful
as a village cricket-green on Sunday." And are these gay
old gentlemen right? Why, provided they are prepared
for death, they *are* a thousand times. Why should they
worry because death seems to be at their door, why
poison life with fear and prudence? Why should they
emulate the old men whom Stevenson pillories, stirring

out from parlours with regulated temperatures only in tin boots, and living on a diet, ever in mortal terror of draughts and microbes? It is better to lose health like a spendthrift than to waste it like a miser.

There are old people who seem to forget they were ever young. They look sourly at the younger generation and speak of it harshly. Yet, no doubt, the youth of every generation has its characteristic faults and failings. It is apt to be rash and irreverent, sensual and fickle, vain, unreasonable, foolish and all the rest of it. The old man has outlived all that, or thinks he has. But are there not characteristic vices of age, too? Is it not too often niggardly, suspicious, cynical, reactionary, and no less selfish than youth? But at least it is prudent. No doubt —with the prudence of the burnt child in the proverb. But, as Stevenson says again, " So soon as prudence has begun to grow up in the brain, like a dismal fungus, it finds its first expression in a paralysis of generous acts." So it is well for the old to recognise betimes the mental or moral maladies that beset their stage of life so that they may vigorously react against all that.

But on the other hand, if it is well that the aged should beware of their own characteristic failings, it is still more important for their happiness that they should realize the privileges and the possibilities of the particular stage in life that they have reached. That the possibilities are there all that I have said in the first part of this chapter goes to show. I could add a great deal by way of showing what people have achieved after they have retired from what seemed to constitute their life-work. But that would be too long a story. Let it suffice for the moment to say that workers in many a noble enterprise and charitable work have been reinforced from the ranks of those who are—presumably—" past their work ". May it long be so.

But what of the compensations, the privileges even, as I have called them, of old age? This is a well-worn theme, yet worth rehearsing. No doubt certain qualities peculiar to youth are gone, not to return, but others abide or have been (often painfully) acquired. Let us think of an ideal old age—we all fall short of it, of course. It has exchanged turbulence for peace, fretfulness for a certain serenity, rawness for mellowness, and is it not Shakespeare who said "ripeness is all"? It is not looking forward to an uncertain and problematical future but back on a very definite past. It has acquired patience. It has achieved tolerance and knows how to make allowances. It is chastened and subdued by life and so is quieter, gentler. If it has really learned the lessons that life ought to teach to anyone, it is humbler, too, and fully aware of its own limitations. Suffering may well have taught it sympathy and kindliness. In short, it has learned many things that youth, on the threshold of life, could not possibly know. And, though the knowledge may be painful, it is salutary.

Let us then not talk of declining years, of going down hill, and of " the sere and yellow leaf ". The bodily powers may wane, but the old head is still wise, the old heart is sound and I hope just a trifle soft. The feelings are under control, the passions subdued. Good work, for others chiefly, may yet be done, if God so will. So, fellow septuagenarians,

> Grow old along with me
> The best is yet to be
> The last of life for which the first was made.

Never forgetting that ' the last of life ' is destined to have an end which is also a beginning, the beginning of that other life which shall never end.

*   *   *   *

A note on some books about old age and an article dealing with certain aspects of it will be found in Appendix B.

EPILOGUE

THERE is a poem of the eighteenth century which, though known by a different title, might well be named 'An Elegy of the People of the Byways'. It was once familiar to all who studied English literature. I wonder if it be still as familiar to any but the elderly. I allude to Gray's Elegy Written in a Country Churchyard. To any who, like the present writer, once knew it all by heart, its lines can hardly fail to come to mind when reflecting on lives that are ordinary, obscure, without distinction or éclat, lives spent in the byways of life.

> Let not Ambition mock their useful toil,
>> Their homely joys and destiny obscure;
> Nor Grandeur hear with a disdainful smile
>> The short and simple annals of the poor.

and not of the poor only but of all who live lives undistinguished and unnoticed amid the mass of mankind.

Passing over the lines, hackneyed by quotation, about the 'flower born to blush unseen', the 'village Hampden' and the 'mute inglorious Milton', we recall the lines that describe so aptly those who feel no yearning for the highways of life but are content to tread its byways all their lives—

> Far from the madding crowd's ignoble strife
>> Their sober wishes never learned to stray,
> Along the cool sequestered vale of life
>> They kept the noiseless tenour of their way.

If what has been written in this little book has interested you, gentle reader (forgive this old-fashioned address), I would ask you to read, whether for the first or for the twentieth time, the whole of Gray's Elegy. And then, when you have read it, I would ask you to turn your thoughts to another life that was passed, nearly all of it, in the byways, or rather in one of the obscurest corners of the world, a spot which, because of that life has become a byword for obscurity and hiddenness— Nazareth of Galilee, for nearly thirty years the dwelling place of Him Whose life was the model for all lives. If you are ever tempted to repine at the ordinariness of your life in the byways, to fret and chafe, perhaps, because your talents are unused and your abilities unrecognized, think of Nazareth and of the Life that was hidden there.

APPENDIX A.

BOOKS ON SELF-DEVELOPMENT.

Self-reverence, self-knowledge, self-control
These three alone lead life to sovereign power.
Yet not for power, (power of herself
Would come uncalled for) but to live by law,
Acting the law we live by without fear;
And, because right is right, to follow right
Were wisdom in the scorn of consequence.

Tennyson: *Oenone.*

The following list of books on subjects dealt with in a preceding chapter is not a bibliography of these subjects. The books mentioned in it are merely samples of a very copious literature. Yet I have thought it well to mention a considerable number of titles, first because of the importance and many sidedness of these subjects, and then because a number of these books are doubtless out of print or otherwise hard to come by, in which case it may be useful to try alternative titles. Books written from a Catholic point of view are indicated by an asterisk*. Not a few of the other books mentioned are from a Christian standpoint, sound on the whole in their outlook. But the inclusion of any book in this list does not amount to a recommendation. The very titles of these books are, however, often suggestive of a line of thought or investigation.

Personality and the Self in General.

"To have personality is simply to be oneself fully and completely. Personality is the synthesis of being. It represents the maximum output of being. To have personality is to get out of ourselves all that is in ourselves. This cannot be done without religion." Father Aloysius Roche: *Religion and Life.*

Le Moi retrouvé. By Père Ch. D. B. Boulogne, O.P. (Lyons: Lardanchet) 1948.

Learn to know oneself by careful study of the working of one's conscience and one's free will. Accept oneself frankly with all one's limitations.

Self-Suggestion. By Canon R. de Saint-Laurent (Dublin: Aubanel) 1950.

,*Personality and Power.* By Shaw Desmond (London: Rockliff 1949.

" Endeavours to demonstrate how necessary a part of civilised life is the effective integration of personality."

How to Succeed. By Rev. Bernard Feeney (New York: Benziger) 4th Edition.

Healthy tone of mind; cheerfulness etc.; curb the passions, mental culture.

Self-Culture. By Dr. Clarke (Boston: Osgood) 1881.

Twenty two lectures embracing every aspect of self-culture " full of ripe experience, profound wisdom, broad views, and religious spirit." The date of this book indicates that systematic self-development is not such a new idea as some people may think.

Personal Psychology. By Morely Dainow (London: Pitman) 1936.

" A practical Guide to self-knowledge, self-development, and self-expression."

Building Personality. By A. Gordon Melvin (U.S.A.: The John Day Co.) 1935.

Good on the practical side.

The Self in Psychology. By A. H. B. Allen (London: Kegan Paul) 1936.

" A study in the foundations of personality ", defending its existence against those who deny it.

Know Thyself. By Burnett Ham (London: Pitman) 1939.

On Being a Real Person. By Harry Emerson Fosdick (London: Student Christian Movement) 4th ed. 1946.

Le Gouvernement de soi-même. By Antonin Eymieu, S.J. 4 vols. (Paris: Perrin).

A work which has passed through a great number of editions.

Vers la Vie pleine à la suite du Père Gratry. By A. Goutay (Paris: Téqui) 1913.

Dwells chiefly, though not exclusively, on the development of the intellect.

A Mirror of Personality. By Rev. John G. Vance (London: Williams and Norgate) 1928.

A book in untechnical language about the discovery of character, temperament, and personality. Catholic viewpoint.

Self-Development. A Handbook for the Ambitious. By H. Addington Bruce (Funk and Wagnall.)

The Making of Personality. 2 Vols. By W. Tudor Jones (London: Williams & Norgate) 1920.

The Cultural Background of Personality. By Ralph Lir ton (London: Kegan Paul) 1948.

Understanding Ourselves. By Mary Macaulay, lecturer in Psychology. (London: Routledge). 1949.

Chapters on marriage, infancy, childhood, and adolescence.

Self Understanding through Psychology and Religion. By Seward Hiltner (London and New York: Scribners) 1951.

Psychology, Religion and Healing. By Rev. Leslie D. Weatherhead (London: Hodder & Stoughton) 1951.

The Gain of Personality. By W. Charles Loosmore (London: Murray) 1930.

" A popular psychological statement of the practical values of personality."

Dimensions of Personality. By H. J. Eysenck (London: Kegan Paul) 1947.

" Findings of a team of psychologists and psychiatrists."

Self-Mastery Through Conscious Auto-Suggestion. By Emile Coué (London: Allen and Unwin) 1945.

Your Psychic Powers and How to Develop Them. By Hereward Carrington (London: Kegan Paul) 1920.

Managing Yourself. By Milton Wright (New York: McGraw Hill) 1938.

The Art of Being a Person. By George Ross Wells (London, New York: Appleton Century) 1939.

Understanding Yourself. By Ernest R. Groves (London: Allen and Unwin) 1936.

" The mental hygiene of personality ", for readers ignorant of psychology.

The Use of the Self. Its conscious direction in relation to Diagnosis, Functioning, and the control of Reaction. (London: Methuen) 1932.

The Art of Creation. Essays on the Self and its Powers. By Edward Carpenter. 1904.

Discovering Ourselves. By Edward A. Strecker and Kenneth E. Appel (N.Y.: Macmillan) 1932.

The Practice of Self-Culture. By Rev. Prof. Hugh Black (London: Hodder and Stoughton) 1908.

Very comprehensive. Culture of body, mind, imagination, heart, conscience, spirit.

Self-Training. The Lines of Mental Progress. By H. Ernest Hunt. (London: Rider) 1918.

Hygiene of the Mind. By Baron Ernst von Feuchters-leben, trans. Sumner (N.Y.: Macmillan Co.) 1934.

**Personality and Successful Living.* By James A. Magner (Milwaukee: Bruce) 1944.

A Catholic work in which the meaning of *Christian* personality is set forth by a well-known writer.

**Personality and its Formation and Action.* By William Healy (N.Y.: Norton) 1938.

This, too, is based on Catholic philosophy.

The Enlargement of Personality. Behaviour Patterns and their Formation. By J. H. Denison (Scribner's) 1931.

**The Significance of Personality.* By Richard M. Vaughan (N.Y.: Macmillan Co.) 1930.

The Crisis of the Human Person. By J. B. Coates (London: Longmans) 1949.

An Exposition of Personalism, the chief protagonist of which was the late Emmanuel Mounier, a Catholic writer.

**Caractère et Personnalité.* By Rev. E. Peillaube. Paris: (Tequi) 1949.

A wise book by a priest who was a professor of Psychology for forty years.

The Mask and the Face. By Kenneth Melvin (London: Methuen) 1948.

" An Introduction to Your Self ".

World Invisible. A study of Personality, by Dallas Kenmare (London: Williams and Norgate) 1950.

" Personality and its relation to the life of the spirit, to love, art, and freedom."

In André Maurois *The Art of Living* there is an excellent chapter on " The Art of Thinking ".

**A Humane Psychology of Education.* By Jaime Castiello, S.J. (London: Sheed and Ward) 1937. Part I: The Raw Stuff of Personality. Part II: The Moulds of Personality. Part III: The Ideal of Personality.

This work is, for the most part, highly technical and employs the technical language—not to say, jargon of modern psychology. From a Christian point of view it is thoroughly reliable.

There is an international quarterly review devoted to our present subject—*Character and Personality.* It is published by George Allen and Unwin, London.

The Mind.

Your Mind and how to Use It. By W. J. Ennever and T. Sharper Knowlson (London: Thorsons) 1947.

The Art of Thought. By Graham Wallas (London: Cape). Stimulating and readable.

Learning to Think. By Lindsay Dewar (London: Rich and Cowan) 1940.

*The Art of Thinking. By the Abbé Ernest Dimnet (New York: Simon and Schuster) 1928.

76,000 copies were sold in the first six months. This is an excellent book, and much practical help may be derived from it.

Use Your Brains. By Dennis Yates and Neil Munro (London: Hutchinson) 1944. Mental Exercises.

*The Intellectual Life. By Père A. D. Sertillanges, O.P. (trans. Prof. M. Ryan) (Cork: Mercier Press).

An analysis of the spirit, conditions, and methods of the intellectual life, with practical conclusions and suggestions.

The Art of Thinking. By T. Sharper Knowlson (London: T. Werner Laurie) new ed. 1918.

*" La Teste bien faicte ". By François Charmot, S.J. (Paris: Spes) 1931.

A study on the training of the mind.

Principles of Mental Development. By Raymond H. Wheeler and Francis T. Perkins (N.Y.: Crowell).

How the Mind Works. By Dr. W. Moodie and Others. (London: George Allen and Unwin) 1934.

Mental Hygiene for Effective Living. By Edwin A. Kirkpatrick (London and New York: Appleton Century) 1935.

Use Your Mind. The Road to successful thinking. By Arnold Hahn (London: Routledge) 1931.

" Nothing if not practical ".

*Directing Mental Energy. By Francis Aveling (University of London Press).

" An attempt to solve in part the problem: ' How can the most be made out of life ' ? "

The Control of the Mind. By R. H. Thouless (London: Hodder and Stoughton) 1928.

" A Handbook of applied psychology for the ordinary man."

*How Our Minds Work. By Mary Dunstan Wilson (Sister of Charity) (Australia) 1925.

An Introduction to Psychology.

Teach Yourself to Think. By R. W. Jepson (London: English Universities Press).

Keeping Mentally Fit. A Guide to Everyday Psychology. By Joseph Jastrow (London: Rider) 1929.

How to Build Mental Power: Concentrating, Developing Judgment, etc. By G. Kleiser (N.Y.: Funk and Wagnall) 1917.

The Reconstruction of Mind. An open way of mind-training. By Esmé Wingfield-Stratford (Liverpool: Books Ltd.) 1921.

The Mind in Daily Life. By R. D. Gillespie, M.D. (London: Methuen) 1933.

Right and Wrong Thinking. By Aaron Martin Crane (Boston: Lothrop, Lee and Shepherd) 1906.

" The undreamt of possibilities which man can achieve through his own mental control."

Mental Life. An Introduction to Psychology. By Beatrice Edgell (London: Methuen) 1926.

A practical book for the student and the general reader.

The Training of Mind and Will. By W. Tudor Jones (London: Williams and Norgate) 1919.

Mental Efficiency. By Arnold Bennett (London: Hodder and Stoughton) N.d. many editions.

How to Use Your Mind. A Psychology of Study. By Harry D. Kitson (N.Y.: Lippincott) 2 ed. 1922.

New Minds for Old. The Art and Science of Mind-Training. By Esmé Wingfield-Stratford (London: Lovat-Dickson) 1934.

A systematic and thorough treatise.

Your Mind and Mine. An Account of Psychology for the Inquiring Layman and the Prospective Student. By Raymond B. Cattell (London: Harrap) 1934.

Mental Training and Efficiency. By F. H. Hayward (London: Sidgwick and Jackson) 1921.

Thought Control in Everyday Life. By James Alexander (London and N.Y.: Funk and Wagnalls).

" Non-technical presentation of psychology applied to mind control, overcoming of bad habits, etc., valuable.

Mental Concentration. By Canon R. de Saint Laurent (Dublin: Aubanel)) 1950.

A practical work written in non-technical language.

Thought the Master-Key. By Leonard F. Jennings (London: Fenland Press) 1933.

Thinking. By H. Levy (London: Newnes) 1936.

" Logic in untechnical terms and some Other Matters."

The Will.

The Education of the Will. By T. Sharper Knowlson.

The author's aim is to set forth in a strictly practical manner the best known methods of developing will-power.

De la Volonté. By M. Duportal (Paris: Lethielleux).

(Crowned by the French Academy). Strongly recommended in Catholic circles.

Le Pouvoir de la Volonté sursoi-même, sur les autres, et sur le destin. By Paul-Clément Jagot. 1921.

The Way to Will Power. By Henry Hazlett (London: Dent) 1932.

Bréviaire de la Volonté. By Jean de Courberive (Avignon: Aubanel) 1950.

La Maîtrise de Soi-même. By J. de Courberive (Paris: Edouard Aubanel) 1935.

A Catholic book (with an Imprimatur) on the training of the will with a view to being " quelqu' un ", i.e., having a real personality.

Le Gouvernement de soi-méme. 3rd Series L'Art de vouloir. By Antonin Eymieu, S.J. (Paris: Perrin).

Strength of Will. By E. Boyd-Barrett (London: Longmans).

The Training of the Will. By John Lindworsky (Milwaukee: Bruce) 1938.

Will-Power. By Canon R. de Saint-Laurent (Dublin: Aubanel) 1950.

Character.

The Psychology of Character. By Rudolf Allers (London: Sheed and Ward) 1931.

The Practical Psychology of Character Development. A briefer and more popular presentation of the previous work (London: Sheed and Ward) 1934.

These two works by an Austrian Professor now teaching in the Catholic University of America are both thoroughly competent and soundly Catholic in outlook.

L'Education et la formation du caractère. By R. P. de Pully, S.J.

Pour être un caractère. By E. Rouzic

The Education of Character. By Father M. S. Gillet, O.P. (London: Washbourne) 1914.

The author of this book was afterwards Master General of the Dominican Order.

Knowledge and Character. By Maxwell Garnett. (Cambridge: University Press).

" His ethic is the Christian ethic, his philosophy the Christian philosophy."—(*Times Literary Supplement*).

The Formation of Character. By E. Hull, S.J.

Christian Character. By Professor T. B. Kilpatrick (Edinburgh: T. and T. Clark).

The Formation of Christian Character. By W. S. Bruce (Edinburgh: T. and T. Clark).

Early Essays and Lectures. By Canon P. A. Sheehan. P. 310. Certain Elements of Character.

Twelve Tests of Character. Essays in Practical Religion and Right Living. By H. Emerson Fosdick.

The Memory.

How to Remember. By Bruno Furst. (London: Thorsons) 1947.

Your Memory. How to Remember and Forget. By Herbert N. Casson (London: Efficiency Magazine) 1930.

Not very deep, not very original.

Best known of memory systems is what is known as Pelmanism.

Comment acquérir une parfaite Mémoire. By Prof. Paul Clément Jagot.

Votre Mémoire. By Paul Nyssens.

The Training of our Faculties in General.

L'Education des Passions. By R. P. Noble, O.P. (Paris: Lethielleux) 1920. Part II of V. Rev. M. S. Gillet, O.P. *The Education of Character* deals with the Passions. (Washbourne, 1915).

Le Bonheur cet inconnu. By R. P. Demarais, O.P. (Paris: Editions Spes) 1950.

Deals with the education of the Imagination, Passions, Memory, Intelligence, and Will.

Méthode progressive et complète de culture psychique. By Canon R. de Saint-Laurent (Avignon: Aubanel) 1950.

Deals with the cultivation and development of all man's powers and faculties.

Deviens un homme. By Jean de Courberive (Avignon: Aubanel) 1950.

**Devenez celui que vous voudriez être par la Psycho-culture.* Same author and publisher. 1950.

APPENDIX B.

1. *Note to Chapter III.*

Self-love and Selfishness.

I have transcribed the following passages with a view to illustrating my chapter " On Making the Most of Oneself ". I do so not because of the authority of these writers but because, from quite different angles, these passages throw light on certain points I tried to make in that chapter which was concluded before I came upon these passages which I owe to Victor Gollancz's anthology *A Year of Grace*. The first passage is from the writings of Sören Kierkegaard, Danish philosopher who, along with much that is for us Catholics unorthodox, wrote also many things that are true and significant. The second is by Peter Wust, a German Catholic professor of philosophy and well known writer. The third is by a contemporary American psychologist of German origin. As for Père Sertillanges, O.P. I have already quoted in Chapter III. from another book of his.

"This was the commandment, "Thou shalt love thy neighbour as thyself ", but when the commandment is rightly understood, it also says the converse, " *Thou shalt love thyself in the right way*." If anyone, therefore, will not learn from Christianity to love *himself* in the right way, then neither can he love his neighbour; he may perhaps, as we say, " for life and death "—cling to one or several other human beings, but this is by no means loving one's neighbour. To love one's self in the right way and to love one's neighbour are absolutely analogous concepts, are at bottom one and the same. When the " as thyself " of the commandment has taken from you the selfishness which Christianity, sad to say, must presuppose as existing in every human being, then you have rightly learned to love yourself. Hence the law is: " You shall love yourself as you love your neighbour when you love him as yourself." Whoever has some knowledge of men will certainly admit that as he has often wished to be able to influence men to give up their self-love, so he has also often wished that it were possible to teach them to love themselves. When the busy man wastes his time and energy on vain and unimportant projects, is this not because he has not rightly learned to love himself? When the frivolous man abandons himself, almost as a mere nothing, to the folly of the moment, is not this because he does not rightly understand how to love himself?

When the melancholy man wishes to be done with life, aye, with himself, is this not because he will not learn strictly and earnestly to love himself? When a man, because the world or another man faithlessly betrayed him, yields himself up to despair, how was he to blame (for we are not here speaking of his innocent suffering), except for not having loved himself in the right way? Ah, and when a man presumptuously lays his hand upon himself, does not his sin precisely consist in not loving himself in the way in which a man *ought* to love himself? Oh, there is so much said in the world about treachery and faithlessness, and, God help us! this is unfortunately only too true, but let us still never forget that the most dangerous traitor of all is the one every man has in his own breast. This treachery, whether it consists in a man's selfishly loving himself, or in the fact that he selfishly does not wish to love himself in the right way, this treachery is certainly a mystery because there is no outcry about it, as is usual in cases of treachery and faithlessness. But is it not therefore all the more important that we should repeatedly be reminded about the Christian teaching: that a man should love his neighbour as himself, that is, as he ought to love himself?"

KIERKEGAARD.

Piety (¹) towards one's self is the great law of love, which we apprehend in the depths of our nature, because each of us is *this* creature who has been given *this* shape and has occupied *this* place in the order of creation; the moment we have apprehended this law, it is incumbent upon us to assert it with all our might. And the bliss of our soul lies in never resisting that silent appeal which mounts up from the depths of our being. . . .

Piety's particular aim is to maintain religious awe in the self towards the metaphysical deeps of its own reality, that mysterious reality with which God has endowed it. For our self is a holy temple of the Spirit, built by God's own hands, a wonderful inner universe with its own laws of gravity, still more marvellous than those we can see in the full vitality of the external universe with its infinity of mechanisms. It is a sanctuary, a Holy of Holies into which we may not enter, though it is ours, without a hidden and holy fear. We *may* not, I said. But also we *cannot*, in this

---

(¹) The word is here used in the original sense of the Latin *pietas*, the nearest English equivalent of which would seem to be ' dutifulness.'

Holy of Holies, enter the place of the altar with the eternal lamp
of the most sacred mysteries burning before it. There is indeed
a sense in which we are given to ourselves. But we are only
entrusted to ourselves as works of art from the studio of an
eternal Master. We are not our *own* masterpieces. That is why
we are only left to ourselves as infinitely precious heirlooms,
which we must treat as we would treat the treasure of our bliss.

PETER WUST.

_____

The assumption underlying the thinking of Luther and Calvin,
and also that of Kant and Freud, is: Selfishness is identical with
self-love. To love others is a virtue, to love oneself is a sin.
Furthermore, love for others and love for oneself are mutually
exclusive.

Theoretically we meet here with a fallacy concerning the nature
of love. Love is not primarily " caused " by a specific object,
but is a lingering quality in a person which is only actualised by
a certain " object ". . . . The basic affirmation contained in
love is directed towards the beloved person as an incarnation of
essentially human qualities. Love for one person implies love for
man as such. Love for man as such is not, as it is frequently
supposed to be, an abstraction coming " after " the love for a
specific person, or an enlargement of the experience with a specific
" object "; it is its premise, although, genetically, it is acquired
in the contact with concrete individuals.

From this it follows that my own self, in principle, is as much
an object of my love as another person. The affirmation of my
own life, happiness, growth, freedom, is rooted in the presence
of the basic readiness of, and ability for, such an affirmation.
If an individual has this readiness, he has it also towards himself.

Selfishness is not identical with self-love but with its very
opposite. Selfishness is one kind of greediness. Like all greediness,
it contains an insatiability, as a consequence of which there is
never any real satisfaction. Greed is a bottomless pit which
exhausts the person in an endless effort to satisfy the need without
ever reaching satisfaction. Close observation shows that while
the selfish person is always anxiously concerned with himself, he
is never satisfied, is always restless, always driven by the fear of
not getting enough, of missing something, of being deprived of
something. He is filled with burning envy of anyone who might
have more. If we observe still closer, especially the unconscious
dynamics, we find that this type of person is basically not fond
of himself, but deeply dislikes himself.

The puzzle in this seeming contradiction is easy to solve. Selfishness is rooted in this very lack of fondness for oneself. The person who is not fond of himself, who does not approve of himself, is in constant anxiety concerning his own self. He has not the inner security which can exist only on the basis of genuine fondness and affirmation. He must be concerned about himself, greedy to get everything for himself, since basically he lacks security and satisfaction

ERICH FROMM

" It is a man's first duty to care for and make the most of himself, since it is only thus he can be fully equipped for the service of others. . . . The goblet must first be full before it can overflow. . . . All helpful love for others begins with a wise and noble love of self."

ROBERT P. DOWNES: *The Art of Noble Living*,
ch. vi. Self-Culture and Noble Living.

Mgr. Fulton Sheen's *Lift Up Your Hearts* (New York: McGraw Hill, 1950) is a sort of informal treatise on psychiatry and in particular the true nature and treatment of the self. And here he makes a very helpful distinction. The self may be lived and may be dealt with on three levels which he names the Ego, the I, and the divine life in us. The ego, " the creation of our mistakes in living ", hides from us our true self, the I, and consequently obscures the image of God in us. We must therefore free ourselves from the bondage of the ego by learning its manifold perversities and how to deal with them. Then and only then can a man foster and develop his true self, his I, achieve self-discipline and build up character. Then, too, he may be ready, and it is to be hoped, willing to co-operate with the grace of God.

Read also *Psychiatry and Asceticism*, by Felix C. Duffey, C.S.C. (St. Louis: Herder, 1950).

" It is enjoined upon us that we should love our neighbour. Now we ourselves are our first neighbour. We are the first territory on which we are to exercise in our human way our divine love.

" ' Self ', we are told, ' is hateful and to be hated '. Most certainly we cannot hate enough the proud self, the pleasure-loving, monopolizing self, the exorbitant self that organizes, carries on, and systematizes in its own interest the bitter struggle for life, the self that by nature—I mean depraved nature—tends to think itself everything both in value and importance

" But that self is not the only one. There is also the sublime and immortal creature which came before the mind of God in His triune solitude, when He said: ' Let us make man '. That is not the hateful self, it is a divine being, since it is the child of God and belongs to His lineage—*Ipsius genus sumus*. We are His very offspring."—[Words of St. Paul at Athens, Acts xvii. 28.]

A. D. SERTILLANGES, O.P., in *L'Amour Chrétién*, ch. vi.

Note to Chapter X.

A further List of Books on Human Suffering.

La Souffrance et Nous. By Père Sanson, the eloquent and moving *conférencier* of Notre Dame (Paris: Flammarion) 1933.

Ma Sœur la Souffrance. By Père Henry Perroy, S.J. (Lyons: Vitte).

Notre Sœur la Douleur. By the Abbé Fumet (Paris) 1938.

La Femme Chrétienne et la Souffrance (Paris: Téqui).

La Divine Douleur. By the poet Francis Jammes (Paris: Bloud et Gay).

Les Douleurs de la Vie. By Mgr. Postel (Paris: Haton).

L' Energie Spirituelle de la Souffrance. By Marguérite-Marie Teilhard de Chardin (Paris: Editions du Seuil, 1951).

The author was helpless and bedridden throughout her life. She became President of the Union Catholique des Malades.

Les Larmes consolées. By Père Charles Laurent, S.M. (Paris: Haton).

Le Psautier de la Bonne Souffrance. By Canon J. M. Lambert (Paris: Spes).

Souffrance, Ecole de Vie. By Suzanne Fouchi (Paris: Spes).

The Craft of Suffering. By Father Vincent McNabb, O.P. (Burns, Oates).

The Joy of Sorrow. By Father David P. McAstocker, S.J. (Milwaukee: Bruce) 1936.

Sown in Tears. Thoughts for Sufferers. By Lady Lovat, with prefatory verses by Aubrey de Vere (Burns, Oates).

Lettres sur la Souffrance. By Elizabeth Leseur (Paris: de Gigord.)

Hope in Suffering. Memories and Reflections of a French Army Chaplain. By Abbé Felix Klein (Melrose, 1916).
De la Douleur. By Mgr. Bougaud. (Paris: de Gigord).
It is noteworthy that some of the above books have passed through many editions amounting to 30,000 or even 50,000 copies.

Note to Chapter XII.

Old Age.

Growing older is an experience that happens and is happening to everybody. It is futile for anybody to pretend that it is not happening to him or to her. To this process of ageing it is well to adjust ourselves gradually, and important to know how to do it. We can learn something from other people around us who have lived long. But often they are not very helpful. We may derive more help and useful suggestions from the few who have devoted special thought and study to the process. One of these is George Lawton. In his book, *Ageing Successfully* (New York: Columbia University Press, 1946) will be found a good deal of sound advice. I am unable, however, to recommend it unreservedly, for it ignores what is the most essential element in life, in age as in youth, religion. But the writer has carried out successfully the aim set forth in his Preface:—

"This volume is a handbook or daily reference guide for the person who sees himself growing older and seeks to exploit the advantage of ageing and to minimize its drawbacks in his own living."

Another book on old age, and one that supplies what is lacking in the book just mentioned, viz., the religious point of view, is *Le Vieillard. La Vie Montante*, by Mgr. Baunard (Paris: de Gigord, 1923). First published in 1910, it had three years later, the sixty-first year of its author's priesthood, reached a seventh edition. I translate the opening sentences which strike the keynote of the book: "To begin with, here is my idea of old age: it is not decline, it is progress; it is not a going down but an ascending. And it is of this ascending life that I wish to describe in this book the boon, the greatness, the high revelations, the intimate joys, and the supreme hope." It is a very beautiful book.

One more reference, it is to *L'Art de Vieillir*, Psychologie Chrétienne de la Vieillesse. By the Abbé J. Brugerette (Paris: Lethielleux).

A SECOND "PRIME OF LIFE"—AFTER 70

Condensed from The New York Times Magazine
MARTIN GUMPERT, M.D.

Author of *You Are Younger Than You Think*, *The Anatomy of Happiness*, etc.

OLD age had long been misinterpreted, clouded by prejudices and conventional assumptions which are the harder to overcome because they have been accepted by the old people themselves throughout their lives. The aged have been considered the inescapable victims of human decline, nearer to death than to life, a sort of refuse which nature would take care of soon enough.

On a recent trip to Europe I visited a number of persons of advanced age, who have actively rejected this traditional concept. They are to me the pioneers of a future type of old person; they are participating creatively in life as long as life lasts.

We think of age 65 as the milestone where active life stops and old age and retirement begin. How arbitrary this artificial signpost is! The youngest person I interviewed in Europe was 77.

In Italy I met 91-year-old Vittorio Emanuele Orlando, the only survivor of the prime ministers who concluded the Treaty of Versailles. He is a small man, but heavy set, with a full crop of white hair—a sort of friendly miniature lion, impulsive and agile. An active member of the Italian Senate, he is head of a successful law firm, president of the Rome lawyers' guild and professor at the University of Rome. In spite of violent political controversies —he is completely independent in his politics—he is treated with reverence as the " grand old man " of Italy. He sleeps well, has never been sick, takes long walks, drinks wine. His greatest friend is his small granddaughter.

Another elderly Italian of incredible vitality is Dr. Raffaele Bastianelli, a surgeon of international reputation. At 87 he operates three times weekly, drives his own car, has daily office hours, does research, and even flew his own plane until five years ago. Bastianelli has had rheumatic arthritis and a bad stomach since he was 30, yet he is a tall, erect man who reads without glasses, whose hands do not show the slightest tremor.

Philosopher Benedetto Croce, 85, lives in the centre of Naples, near the Italian Institute of Historical Studies which he founded and which houses his wonderful library and a lecture room where he teaches. He gets up at 8 a.m. and works for ten hours. He eats very little—no meat—but seems well nourished and looks like a kindly old walrus. Croce suffered a stroke last year but has completely recovered—he speaks, hears and writes without diffi-culty. He, too, is active as a Senator and is of inexhaustible productivity. Two books by him were published in 1950; a new book of his philosophical essays is almost ready.

Bernhard Berenson, the art historian, 86, lives near Florence, surrounded by the most exquisite samples of Florentine painting, Asiatic and Egyptian sculpture, and a well-organized library of 50,000 books. He has just published a book on the painter Caravaggio. Another book is ready for publication. If only, he says, he could stand at a corner with his hat and beg people to throw him their wasted hours.

George Santayana, the philosopher, 88, has lived for the past ten years in Rome. His eyesight is failing but his work goes on, and he showed me the proofs of a voluminous new book. He reads Latin literature, is highly interested in modern poetry.

Edouard Herriot of France has just turned 79. He wakes at 7 a.m., has breakfast in bed and works until 10 or 11. On three days he presides at the National Assembly; he is also president of his Radical Socialist Party. He sees countless official visitors. Every Saturday morning he drives to Lyons, of which he is the mayor. He spends Sunday with his wife in an old castle, Monday in his town house and with the city council. On Tuesday he goes back to Paris. He writes two articles every month, is preparing the second volume of his memoirs, and in 1949 finished a book on Rodin. He loves music and the theatre, goes twice a month to the Comédie Française, and his greatest enjoyment is regular attend-ance at the circus, accompanied by small children. With all this goes a phlebitis of his left leg and chronic bronchitis.

In England there is Viscount Samuel, former British High Commissioner of Palestine, now 81, who has just published a work that deals with the interrelation of science, philosophy, and religion. " This book wrote itself ", he said. " It was a new subject to me. But the older I grow the easier I find the flow of ideas."

There is Bertrand Russell, preparing his autobiography at 79 and complaining that he is easily tired because he cannot walk more than five miles at a time. There is Lord Horder, a physician to the King, whom I visited in his Harley Street office the day after his 80th birthday. He puts in 12 hours of work daily, and writes poetry and takes care of his garden in his leisure time.

Among the notable women I talked with was Dr. Helen A. Boyle of Brighton, 81, the first woman president of the Royal Medico-Psychological Association. She practices psychiatry in London and Brighton and is now interested in founding a centre to promote collaboration between clergy and physicians. Dr. Boyle eats what she likes, drinks enormous quantities of tea—and small ones of whisky—sleeps one hour in the afternoon and goes to bed at 2 a.m.

There is no fixed rule of physical behaviour for a long and successful life; some of the persons I interviewed had never been seriously ill, some had been sick throughout their lives. Some are well-to-do, some are poor; but none of them seemed to be degraded by extreme poverty, none spoiled by extreme riches.

All of them seemed to enjoy their lives far beyond the average middle-aged individual, and none seemed afraid of death. They seemed to have a need for human warmth, human contact, for being talked to. Yet none showed the features of bitter despair and retardation which we so often encounter in older people; all of them were kind and thoughtful and emotionally sensitive. The most frequent complaint was a deficient memory for names.

All of these people have unceasingly used their intelligence, have continued to learn and to grow. They have never narrowed their interests; they are " modern " in the best sense of the word. The most constructive impression I had is that old age develops a creative urge and power of its own, of which we have hardly taken notice up to now.

Almost daily, among the old people I meet, I observe this need to create, this sudden wave of emotions, this craving for knowledge and human growth. Such enlargement of their existence has often developed, to their own surprise, for the first time in their lives. And I wonder whether life as a whole will not be richer and happier for all of us once we start discovering the unknown treasures of old age, now hidden under old age's miseries.

We sometimes call an old man's dotage " second childhood ". I suggest that there is often, instead, a second prime of life which we should discover and explore and cherish.